I FOUGHT THE LAW:

THE LIFE AND STRANGE DEATH OF BOBBY FULLER

I FOUGHT THE LAW:
THE LIFE AND STRANGE DEATH OF BOBBY FULLER

by

MIRIAM LINNA

and

RANDELL FULLER

KICKS BOOKS
NEW YORK, NEW YORK

Copyright © 2014 by Kicks Books

All images are courtesy Bobby Fuller Archive@ Kicks Books unless credited otherwise.

All rights reserved. No part of this book shall be reproduced, stored in a retrieval system, or transmitted by any means – electronic, mechanical, photocopying, recording, or otherwise – without written permission from the publisher.

Published in 2014 by Kicks Books
PO Box 646 Cooper Station
New York NY 10276

Printed in the United States of America

ISBN: 978-1-940157-11-5

Also available as print edition from kicksbooks.com

Editor: Miriam Linna
Design: Patrick Broderick/Rotodesign

www.kicksbooks.com

*This book is dedicated
to my brother Bobby
and to our mother and father,
Loraine and Lawson Fuller*

—R.F.

ALSO FROM KICKS BOOKS

SWEETS by Andre Williams
THIS PLANET IS DOOMED by Sun Ra
SAVE THE LAST DANCE FOR SATAN by Nick Tosches
PULLING A TRAIN by Harlan Ellison
LORD OF GARBAGE by Kim Fowley
GETTING IN THE WIND by Harlan Ellison
GONE MAN SQUARED by Royston Ellis
BENZEDRINE HIGHWAY by Charles Plymell
PROPHETIKA BOOK ONE by Sun Ra
PLANET PAIN by Kim Fowley
STREETS by Andre Williams
SWEET EBONY by Royston Ellis
RUSH AT THE END by Royston Ellis
MALDIVES ADVENTURE by Royston Ellis

CONTENTS

Introduction by Randy Fuller IX
THE LAW WAS A GIANT 8-BALL by Tiger Moody XI
PROLOGUE by Randy Fuller XVII
CHAPTER ONE: BEGINNINGS 1
CHAPTER TWO: COOL IT 21
CHAPTER THREE: THUNDER 36
CHAPTER FOUR: JUAREZ 43
CHAPTER FIVE: THE LOST GOLDMINE 48
CHAPTER SIX: ONLY FOR YOU 60
CHAPTER SEVEN: WINTER SURFIN' 73
CHAPTER EIGHT: STRINGER 89
CHAPTER NINE: TEENAGE HEAVEN 111
CHAPTER TEN: OUR FAVORITE MARTIAN 120
CHAPTER ELEVEN: LET HER DANCE 130
CHAPTER TWELVE: HOLLYWOOD A GO-GO 151
CHAPTER THIRTEEN: THE MAGIC TOUCH 177
INTERVIEW WITH BOBBY & RANDY FULLER 233
DISCOGRAPHY 238

First of all I would like to thank God, for getting me through this. I would like to thank all the fans who have stuck by me all these years—Jeannie, thank you for your encouragement and prayers, pictures and memories, and thank you to Charlene, who so generously shared personal memories and photographs. I would like to thank everyone who shared their stories. Thank you, Miriam Linna for giving me the opportunity to do this. I wouldn't have wanted to do this with anyone else. Thank you for all your hard work. I know you put your heart into this. Thank you for your support and friendship all these years. Thank you to my wife Dale, you never doubted me, when I doubted myself, you have always been my biggest cheerleader. Thank you to my daughters, who also cheered me on.

—Randy Fuller

INTRODUCTION
by RANDY FULLER

I was inspired to write this book with Miriam Linna for several reasons. For all these years I have kept this pain locked up deep inside me. In telling my story, I hoped that I could release all the pain and heartache once and for all. Bobby's death not only broke my heart, it also shattered all of our dreams. I wanted to clear up rumors and untruths. I wanted everyone to know what it was like to grow up with Bobby and about the dreams that we shared, and how suddenly it was all gone.

This slim volume has been in the making for quite a while. It began as a story in Kicks Magazine back in 1988, and like most all stories in Kicks, it has grown with each new character coming into play, each new scrap of information or lost recording entering its orbit. I owe a true debt of gratitude to all members of the Fanatics and the Bobby Fuller Four, living and otherwise, and to everyone who participated herein. Thank you. Dewayne Quirico, you are amazing and I thank you and Joyce for your birdseye views. Thank you to Ana Economou, Gianni Himmel, and Billy Miller for help with tape transcriptions. Thanks also to Pathologist Mark E. Smethurst, M.D., Nila Onuferko, Bob Santos, Liam O'Malley and Mel Bergman.

Randy Fuller, thank you for never mincing words and for laying your heart on the line. This is your story. It has been a privilege. Thank you also to the fantastic Dale Fuller, and to Howie Pyro for the friendship and the fanship, and the great road tripping experiences, to Pat Broderick for the magic eye and perseverance, to Tammy for limitless patience and consideration, and especially to my better half, Billy Miller, who continues to share in this rock and roll adventure with all pistons firing.

—M.L.

THE LAW WAS A GIANT 8-BALL
by TIGER MOODY

Bobby Fuller fought the law and the law won. But the law wasn't a fat man in creased gabardine and a Stetson. The law was a giant 8-ball, speeding across the felt, flattening every poor fool in its path.

I recall one muggy Friday night, years ago, when I was still just knee-high to a bandit coon. My stepfather Tom and I were sitting in the unpainted pine bleachers of a dusty speedway on the outskirts of a town whose zoning board seemed to stipulate that every house provide a snarling Doberman chained to its porch. Tom, a large, scary man, had been a drag racing greaser-type in his youth. He was the first Bobby Fuller fan I'd ever known, and he'd often pluck away at *I Fought The Law* on his cheap plywood acoustic, when he was drunk enough to forget to be hard.

The speedway stands were rife with drunkards, untamed moustaches, shapeless, quivering breasts, and profanities of types still mysterious to me. The stock cars on the track were loud, angry, and unsavory. Tom gargled his Schlitz like mouthwash to make me laugh. He spat beer against my shaggy mane and shampooed it into my scalp with a calloused, meaty left palm. He handed me the large wax cup and I sipped at the foam sheepishly.

"Good, eh Tiger? Drink some more. There ya go, good boy..."

I was eight years old.

We watched the battered, matte primered beasts go 'round and around and around in silence, Tom too entranced by the blurs and snarls for casual conversation. I didn't really know what was going on. I'd never been to a speedway before. I was a faggy, borderline-effete kid, more into Three Stooges shorts, German Expressionist paintings, and the French Revolution than anything as manly as pistons or sparkplugs. But Tom was undaunted; he was determined to make a man out of me. He'd shown me how to build a zip gun the week before.

At one point, Tom placed a hand on my shoulder. His voice was slurred with beer and disappointment, his eyes dreamy and sad.

"Tiger, all I really wanna do in life is to race here someday. Just once. Tell me...is that asking too fucking much?"

I remained silent, I wasn't sure if that was a trick question.

After a while, Tom shoved a crumpled five dollar bill my way and ordered me down to the concession-stand for hot dogs, pretzels, and more beer.

I stared at the strange grown-ups around me, mostly blue-collar types in various stages of inebriation. In front of me was a young couple, both tall and long-haired, reeking of things that I'd later realize belonged to marijuana and sex. I listened to them joke and laugh and watched in awe as they leaned towards each other and slowly tongue-kissed.

I'd never seen anything like it and I found it disgusting; but it was hard not to absorb the profound waves of happiness they emanated. I'd never seen two people as happy to be in each other's presence, ever. This was what love looked like. I'd been a bitter, unhappy child for as long as I could remember; obsessed with darkness, death, and doom. These beautiful people filled me with a glimmer of hope. Maybe things could get better. Maybe things could change. Maybe I *could* win.

The line moved quickly, and soon it was my turn. Tom's tired five-dollar bill enabled me to purchase three hot dogs, two pretzels, and a large cup of beer with some change leftover. I asked for some mustard and the spotty vendor pointed at a thin counter around the side of the trailer.

The counter was guarded by a swarm of buzzing horseflies. I couldn't reach the mustard-pump. I placed a hot dog at the base of the crusty tub and tried jumping up to smack its pommel, but it was no use. I heard a woman's voice behind me.

"Need a lift, little man?"

It was her, the tongue-kisser. She was wearing a tight, yellow, long-sleeved blouse. She'd forgotten to wear a bra.

She lifted me with her hands around my waist, her red fingernails digging into my soft sides while I worked the mustard-pump over the dogs and pretzels. She set me down gently and I thanked her. I didn't mind her stench. Her boyfriend asked me if he could have a bite of my weiner. He was wearing a t-shirt with a thick, rubbery Stars and Bars transfer. Above the flag was a banner that read 'American by Birth.' The banner beneath the flag read 'Southern by Grace of God.' Even as a small child, this struck me as a strange thing to wear in the Northeast; but, to be fair, we were in the South of New Jersey. I nodded again and handed him a hot dog. He engulfed eighty five percent of it with one chomp and handed me back the stump. Then he draped his arm around his girl like a sleeping python and they sauntered off laughing. I stared at the stump, ate it, and returned to the bleachers.

Three races later, on the opposite side of the track, a car spun out of control, its rear wheel flying loose into the stands. There was too much dust, smoke and general commotion to make out the details of what was happening, but still I craned my neck to try. There were screams, both of fear and agony. Several people lay motionless on the stands as their neighbors parted. Tom grabbed me and began dragging me down the stands along with the rest of the frantic spectators.

As we shuffled out of the speedway with the crowd, Tom shouted into my right ear. He reminded me that, if probed, to stick to our lie and tell my mother that we had indeed gone to the movies.

The girl from the mustard-pump was outside of the gate, leaning against the chickenwire, heaving with hysterical sobs. She was by herself. I began to move towards her to ask what was wrong when Tom snagged the back of my collar and yanked me along with him. When I protested, he backhanded me across the mouth, splitting my lip with his chunky class ring.

I stared at the girl as I was dragged away. She didn't appear injured, but her blouse was glued to her breasts with blood. There was blood on her face and in her hair too.

We drove home in utter silence. I'd tried to turn the radio on, but Tom slapped my hand away from the dial. Ten minutes later, he honked at a wild turkey parked in the middle of the road. It galloped wildly out of our path and straight into that of a microbus headed south in the opposite lane. I didn't see the collision, but I heard the thump. After a while, I worked up the courage to ask Tom if I could please put the radio on, and this time he acquiesced. *A Boy Named Sue* was playing. As Tom softly tapped out the rhythm on the steering wheel, the tension gradually eased. He sighed and looked at me.

"Tiger, don't forget. We went to the movies, and if your ma asks you what happened, just say the good guy won."

I said okay and we kept driving. Five minutes passed and he spoke again.

"I'm real sorry that you had to see that tonight, Tiger. But there's one thing you can take away from it: when your fucking number's up...well, then it's fucking up."

I nodded and mulled Tom's words. I wasn't certain whether he was referring to the injured spectators or the turkey. To be honest, I'm still not sure.

When we arrived home, Mom was in the living room laying across the couch smoking a Kools and watching *Nightline*. She glanced at my bloody mouth, shrugged, and asked me how the movie was. Tom watched carefully for my response. I wiped at my eyes and mustered my bravest smile.

"It was great."

Later, I heard Tom through my thin bedroom door, plucking away at his cheap guitar.

>they don't think they're too smart or desperate
>they know that the law always wins
>They've been shot at before
>but they do not ignore
>that death is the wages of sin

These words were written in 1933 by another young Texan. Her name: Bonnie Parker. Like Bobby Fuller, she died bleeding in a car at twenty three. And, like Bobby, she made sure to leave her mark in the world first. My stepfather Tom died in a car too, his heart expiring in the parking lot of a White Castle franchise in Passaic; his only company the fifteen empty slider boxes on the passenger's seat.

He never did get to race that junker.

PROLOGUE 1966
by RANDY FULLER

The blacktop stretched in a straight line through the New Mexico desert into a hazy oblivion. I had been elected to drive Mom's Oldsmobile home to Texas after the funeral. She and Dad had flown home, and later Dad said Mom had to be restrained, because she was out of her mind with grief and trying to jump off the plane.

The "88" was towing an overloaded trailer packed with all of Bobby's stuff—instruments, amps, records, clothes, everything. Mom wanted to take it all back home. I don't know what for. This older couple, friends of my parents, the Pierces, were along for the ride back to El Paso. They didn't want me driving all the way back alone. They were just laying in pools of sweat in the back seat, pretty much. I looked in the rear view mirror and Mrs. Pierce had her head back, mouth open, catching flies. A hot wind was blowing the car and trailer around real bad. Even with the 394-cubic-inch Rocket V8 engine going full tilt, we'd nearly turned over a couple of times, with that trailer pulling in all directions.

There was nothing but sand in all directions outside, and inside the car, it was like a pressure cooker waiting to blow. The A/C wasn't doing a damn thing, and the car was starting to smell of gasoline coming up off the seats and floor. I had the radio going, and when the news came on, they said the temperature was 111 degrees, like that was nothing special.

Normally, without a load, you could drive the 800 mile distance between LA and El Paso in twelve hours. At the rate we were going, it was going to be tomorrow before we got into Texas.

The car stank of gas something terrible now. I kept going over things in my head. Blood all over the seat. The gas can. The worn slippers. His face, all covered with oozing red blisters.

I had put papers down over the bloody bench seat so the Pierces didn't have to look at it. Bobby's head and face had been way down in the crack of the seat, and he bled from the face there. They had pulled him right out backwards, the cops, that is—they just pulled him right out of the car head first. You could see it on TV, it was on the news, showing them pulling his body out of the car and sticking it into the coroner's vehicle. I think they just thought he committed suicide and that was it and they didn't do anything else about it. A lot of musicians committed suicide back then, I guess because of drugs, or a few anyway…

The gas stink was getting unbearable and now there was something worse going on that no amount of air conditioning was going to be able to help. I opened my window and a huge blast of hot air tore in and whipped up the newspapers I had jammed into the passenger seat to cover the blood. The stained papers fluttered around the car in a whirlwind and slapped into Mrs. Pierce's face. She let out a scream like some kind of wild animal. It scared the hell out of me, and suddenly I see some drunk coming down the wrong side of the highway and I swerved to the other side holding that wheel with everything I could muster. The car and trailer came to a stop on the dirt shoulder, setting off a giant cloud of dust. The car radio was blaring. Mrs. Pierce was still screaming and the car seemed to fill with the smell of death. I got the door open and made it out a few steps into the desert before I fell on my knees, retching. Now both the Pierces were crying and I heard Mr. Pierce say "Oh, Lord" a few times so I knew he was praying. Or maybe he was cursing. The sun was burning a hole into my head as I turned to find my way back into the car. I fell into the seat and went to full the door shut, immediately feeling my flesh fry and the touch of the metal handle. I pulled away, howling, and knew I was about to cry like a baby.

As though on cue, the radio started blasting *I Fought The Law*.

CHAPTER ONE

BEGINNINGS

The story of the Rock and Roll King of the Southwest begins years before he was a twinkle in his mother's eye. Both parents had come from broken marriages, with children. It would be several years before the birth of their sons, Robert and Randell, but once the boys had arrived, their lives had meaning and focus. Randell—Randy Fuller—begins his Texas saga.

RANDELL FULLER

My father, Lawson Fuller, met my mother Eva Loraine Barrett, in 1936, in a coffee shop in Big Spring, Texas where she was waiting tables. They fell in love right away and got married. Mother had been married previously to a young man in El Paso by the name of Tommy Leflar, who she loved very much. Tommy had a serious drinking problem though, and Mother couldn't take the abuse. She took their young son, Doras Franklin, nicknamed Jack, and left. A few years later, Tommy would die from tuberculosis and alcohol related illness. After that, Mother swore she would never set foot in El Paso again.

Before he met my mother, my dad was working in the shipyards in Corpus Christi. He was married to a woman named

LEFT: *Mildred and Bill Barrett;*
RIGHT: *Joyce, Jack and Donnell Fuller*

Mittie, and they were having difficulty in their marriage, which led to a divorce. They had two children, Joyce and Donnell. Mittie married my dad's boss, Edale Snell as soon as she could. Joyce and Donnell lived with them, but Dad had visitation rights. My half brother Donnell, who I never got to know, was very popular in school, and what I heard from my sister Joyce was that he was very much like my father. One day, Edale and Donnell were on their way to an oil well. Edale was driving at a high rate of speed and lost control of the car. It flipped over and Donnell lay crushed under it. He died later that day in the hospital. He was fifteen. That was in August of 1941. Dad was devastated, but being very strong, he didn't let it destroy him. Dad was a very proud and outspoken man, with a deep voice, and yes, he had that John Wayne-type personality. Donnell's death had a lot of influence on the way my dad would raise me and Bobby.

Mother and Dad were married for six years before Bobby arrived. Mother's son Jack was their only child all that time. Dad had gotten an offer to work in the oil fields in Midland-Odessa

LEFT: *Lawson and Loraine;*
RIGHT: *Randy and Bobby*

and other areas in Texas, wherever there was drilling of new wells. It paid good money, so he gladly took the job, although he was always on the go. Dad did well at it, and with a lot of hard work he became a tool pusher, hiring and firing roughnecks as he worked up the ranks, drilling for oil and gas.

About a year after losing Donnell, on October 22, 1942, Bobby was born in Goose Creek, Texas where Dad was working at that time. After a year or so, he and Mother and Bobby and Jack, who was about thirteen at the time, moved to where Dad was set up in the Panhandle, close to Hobbs, New Mexico. That's where I was born, on January 29, 1944.

Our step-brother Jack had been arguing and fighting a lot with Dad. Mainly to keep him busy and out of trouble, Dad got Jack work in the oil fields. That worried mother because of the dangers in the fields. Jack hated the greasy work and got in fights with the other hands and drillers, and eventually, he got fired. Whenever Dad tried to correct him, Jack

I FOUGHT THE LAW

would go to my grandparents' farm in Plainview and stay there until things cooled down. But as the story goes, they all felt sorry for Jack, being as he didn't have his real dad all those years. Our grandparents—they were Jack's grandparents too- Mother's mom and dad—well, they spoiled him and made it look like our dad was the bad guy. According to Dad. It made for a real bad situation and caused a lot of stress on Mother and Dad's relationship. Then, Jack's real dad Tommy died in 1944 from TB. That made things worse for him, I think.

Jack went and joined the Navy, I guess to escape the tension. He served his time and in 1947, received an honorable discharge. When he got out, he came back to work in the oil fields, and the problems started all over again. He had to spend a few months at a mental institution to keep from going to jail. He put on an act that he was mentally unstable, and the court went for it. The pain was almost unbearable for Mother, but she survived it. When Jack was released, he came back to Odessa and Dad got him a job in the oil fields again and everything was going good. He seemed to have learned his lesson.

LEFT: *Loraine and Lawson;*
RIGHT: *Pony Express*

I FOUGHT THE LAW

We moved to Lubbock in 1950. I suppose it was better for Mother to be close to her relatives who were a short drive away in Plainview. Dad was gone most of the time, out of town working. He was still within driving distance to the oil wells, but usually he stayed at the rig's bunkhouse for several days at a stretch. I remember one of many stories Dad told about how a roughneck worker used to tease all the other hands by putting things like harmless animals or insects in a new guy's shoes, just to scare the crap out of him. There were a lot of rattlesnakes that would get up in the drill pipes. A few workers had been bitten. So you could imagine what effect a gag like that had on a greenhorn. One time, some new boy got even and tied a two foot piece of rope in the overalls of the guy that had been teasing the new boys. When he put them on, he felt the rope down by his privates and began to sweat. He then grabbed his crotch and hung on to the rope for dear life, and hollered "there's a snake in my overalls. Somebody hand me their knife so I can cut him outta here before I get bit." My dad trying to hold back the laughter, and handed him his knife, and the rough neck proceeded to cut a nice big hole in

LEFT: *Playing in the yard, Hobbs, NM;*
RIGHT: *Loraine Fuller with Randy and Bobby, 1948*

his brand new overalls. Then he grabbed the rope and pulled it out, saw it was a rope, and said, kinda slow, with a south Texas drawl, "why you sorry son of a bitch."

Life in Lubbock was pleasant. Things were going okay. Mother seemed very happy and Bobby was starting first grade at George R. Bean Elementary School while I was starting kindergarten there. Just for the record, Buddy Holly was in high school in town at the same time. We had lived in Lubbock for about two years, when Dad got an offer to move to Farmington, New Mexico, where they had discovered oil and gas in the San Juan Basin. With his drilling experience, he got a supervisor job with the El Paso Natural Gas Company. I do believe this was the happiest time in my life. Farmington! What a place for a young boy to grow up—a boomtown in the middle of nowhere. Farmington had the personality of the Old West with Indians and cowboys, hunting and fishing, virgin wilderness. The vast plains with wild Indian ponies with their long winter coats being herded by a young buck Navajo or Apache covered with a beautiful Indian blanket to keep him warm. Shiprock and the Aztec ruins in the distance, old hogans on top of what they called the bluffs, where you could find arrowheads and other artifacts if you had a mind to. The San Juan River and the Animas River where you could ride the rapids on a large hunk of driftwood, like my best friend Roy Lee Raines and I did.

Jack came to Farmington to be close to us, and to get back to working in the oil fields. Not long after his return, he came to our house late one night that Dad was out of town. I woke up when I heard him yelling, "I'm going to kill those dirty S.O.B.'s!" Jack had blood all over him, and pieces of skin torn from his face. Mother was crying and screaming hysterically, "Jack, stay here, they'll kill you, please don't go!" He'd been in a fight with several roughnecks after work. They had beat him with the same chains they used on the rigs. Jack had learned to take care of himself pretty good and he was tall and lanky and very strong, but it's hard to win a fight when five or six good old boys start beating on you with four foot coupling chains.

Dad told me a story about Jack. He was at a night club on the outskirts of Farmington, called the El Vasita, nicknamed The Bloody Bucket, when some of the hands that worked under my dad were there drinking. They were really lowering the boom on Dad. Jack overheard them talking, and said, "You boys better stop knocking my dad, or I'm gonna make you eat those words." Then the brawl began. The bartender was a friend of my dad, and he said, "I was gonna jump in and help Jack, but by the time I got around the bar, Jack had laid all five of them out." The bartender later told Dad, "I ain't never seen nobody fight like that," and Dad had said, "I sure wish I could have been there."

My half sister Joyce lived in Farmington also, with her husband Lee Rather and my niece, Daranda. Lee was in the oil business, with a company called Halliburton. Like my dad, he was transferred from the Midland-Odessa area because of the oil boom in the San Juan Basin—just one big happy family. Farm-

LEFT: *Randy*; CENTER: *Bobby*;
RIGHT: *Wheels*

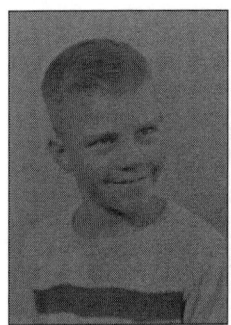 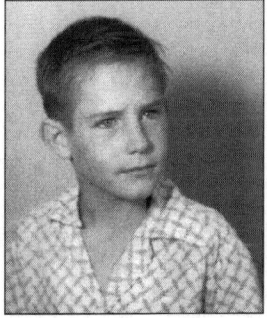 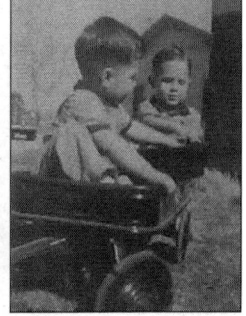

ington was the beginning of Bobby's musical life. Mine, too. He was already playing cornet at school. We both took piano lessons, but having more confidence, and being the oldest, Bobby excelled, while I became more and more insecure, believing I could never be as good as him. When company would come over, Dad would make a big issue about how we were doing in our lessons. The company would just have to hear a recital. First Bobby'd play the cornet, then the piano.

Bobby became obsessed by the attention and made teasing remarks to me about how much better he was than I. Typical brotherly love. Mom and Dad felt bad for me, and would try to get me to play for the guests, but by that time it was too late—the damage had been done. Bobby became more and more interested in different ways to entertain. He started learning the ukulele and bought a dummy that would sit on his lap, and he would throw his voice to make it look like the dummy was talking. The dummy looked kind of like Howdy Doody. The dummy act was another big hit with company.

Mother also played the piano. Actually she was very good. She could really play songs like *Down Yonder* with a lot of white

LEFT: *Hats make the man;*
CENTER: *Bobby gets the gall girl;*
RIGHT: *Bobby and Randy as hepcats*

man soul. Dad, too, loved music, and could hit a few bluegrass songs like Turkey in the Straw on the fiddle. He could really make you laugh. I think Dad should have pursued an acting career. He only went to the eighth grade, because of having to work on the farm, picking cotton, plowing the fields and taking care of animals, but you would think he had a college education in geology or archeology as he progressed in the oil business.

In around 1954, it was time for another promotion. Dad was offered a new position with a raise in Salt Lake City, Utah. It sure was hard to say goodbye to good old Farmington. We were worried that no place could ever take its place. Not to mention my very best friend, Roy, the next best thing to Johnny Sheffield, Tarzan's boy. After throwing tantrums and crying about leaving, Mother turned on the car radio and Elvis was singing *"That's All Right"*. We got excited—we'd never heard that kind of singing before. I forgot about having to move, and said, "Now that is what I want to do someday." Bobby, said, "Yeah, that'll be the day. Your eyes are sunk back in your head too far, and you don't have enough intelligence." Dad had to break up the fight. Another kick in the old insecure ass again. I just wonder how many boys said they would like to sing like Elvis and their brother told them they didn't have enough intelligence. Boy, did he have my number. It pissed me off and I was beginning to think it was true. One thing about the drive from Farmington to Salt Lake City is there is a lot of beautiful scenery, and at least that part of the move was bearable.

When we pulled into Salt Lake, we all knew we were going to like it. It was such a wonderful clean city at that time. The Mormons took good care of it. We settled into a motel, and began searching for a home. We found this really nice house that had a large back section where you could have chickens or horses or cows. Way in the back was this beautiful cemetery full of blue spruce, pines, and chestnut trees. The house itself had a large basement where Bobby and I made our bedrooms. Perfect for young boys. Funny, after all this time I can still remember the strange address: 1570 East 3350 South.

In no time we started making friends and getting ready to start school. Grade school there was perfect for anyone interested in music because Salt Lake grade schools at that time didn't have sports other than track, so you either played music or ran track. And I don't have to tell you what Bobby and I did. Salt Lake was known at that time for basketball, track and Jazz. That was the beginning of us getting serious in music. Bobby decided he was going to play trumpet and so he was put in the band. Mom and Dad talked me into playing the trombone and said I could be like Tommy Dorsey. So that is what I did, but there was no room in the band so they put me in the orchestra. Somehow I didn't seem to fit. The director set me down next to this kid who had been studying trombone, I believe, coming out of the womb. That kid could flat play. It was like having Bobby playing next to me—Insecure City. The bad thing about the situation was that I didn't know one thing about the trombone, so when the orchestra began to play I would just try to move my slide the same way he did while looking out the corner of my eye. Boy did that get some dirty looks, and my face turned many shades of red. He was already on to another note when I was reaching the note he just left. I can't remember how long this went on but it was pure hell. Bobby on the other hand, decided to take up the drums and he became one of the best drummers, if not the best drummer, in all of Salt Lake. When he started high school at Granite High in 1957, he played in a jazz trio in a coffee house, which actually was another name for a beatnik joint in those days.

I FOUGHT THE LAW

LEFT: *Little big men, 1946;* CENTER: *Bobby, 1951*
RIGHT: *Backyard fun*

I will never forget that Bobby didn't want my dad to know he was playing there. Dad thought he was really playing at a cafe. When he found out what it really was, he blew his stack. He wanted us to play music but he didn't want us to have a nightclub musician's life style. We all got a kick out of Dad. He had gotten out of sync with the new generation. Bobby progressed so fast on the drums that his teacher was trying to talk Mom and Dad into sending him to the Julliard School of Music when he was old enough. They said he had that special gift. Woe was me!

Bobby ended up playing drums in a jazz group with a gifted piano player by the name of Larry Jackstein, who later, after we moved to El Paso, got a job doubling duets in concerts with George Shearing.

Well, it was about time for our big brother Jack to come to Salt Lake to visit for a while. I know it was sometime after the fourth of July, because Bobby and me were telling Jack about some cracker balls that we had had fun with on the holiday. We could throw them at each other and they didn't hurt too bad. Our friends and us would choose up sides and have ourselves a little wartime. We told Jack that we were going to try to make some, but all we had was a chemistry set that Mom and Dad got us for Christmas. Jack laughed and said, "That reminds me of that time we were having that family reunion

I FOUGHT THE LAW

LEFT: *Randy and Bobby;*
RIGHT: *Bobby on horseback*

with Mom at Barrett's farm." The Barretts were our grandparents on Mother's side. Two of our cousins who lived on a farm not far from Grandma and Grandpa got Bobby, Jack and me to go swimming in some caliche pits that some construction company had made while blasting. These were deep pits that had filled with water that fed into the pits from, I think, underground springs. The water was crystal clear with a tint of cobalt blue—very good swimming for a bunch of young Tom Sawyer and Huckleberry Finn types! Right next to the pits was a shack, and my cousin went over to investigate, found the door was unlocked, and went in. What do think he found? Well, there was a stack of boxes of dynamite and caps which we found irresistible, so we borrowed a couple boxes. After that we took off to the boonies so we could blow some holes in the ground, plus a few trees. When we got there, my cousin said, "Oh, no! We don't have any way of setting off the caps."

Jack said, "Don't worry boys, I'll show you how a pro does it." Jack had done a lot of demolition work in the Navy and in the oil fields working on the derricks. He said, "Randell, get my flashlight from the glove box, and that roll of electrical wire from the tool box in my trunk." Then he ran two wires from the dynamite and cap back to the two flashlight batteries, touched the negative, then the positive, and BOOM! We had a ball! It was getting close to midnight, so we decided we had better get back home. On the way, we went through this small town called Kress, a little dry Baptist farm town where everyone went to bed no later than nine o'clock. There wasn't a light on anywhere. Jack stopped the car and with a grin said, "Lets go back to Kress and wake those holy rollers up."

We turned around and drove right into the middle of downtown. Jack got out and set five sticks of dynamite down about thirty feet from the car, got the flashlight batteries out, touched the negative then the positive, and, well—BOOM! One by one, house by house, the little town of Kress awoke. We got real scared, put the car in low, and burned rubber all the way out of town. Thank God we made it back to the farm, where we got a good lecture about being late at the family reunion.

The next morning it was on every radio station and local TV, pleading for whoever took the dynamite and caps, to please return it with no questions asked, because just the caps alone could dismember or kill you. Thank God we left for home that next day. I think my cousins took what was left of the dynamite and caps back, saying they found them alongside a country farm road. Later on my cousins learned how to make their own gunpowder out of saltpeter, sulfur, and powdered charcoal—barbecue briquettes worked fine if you powdered them in a mortar and pestle. Since they had welders on the farm, they even fabricated their own cannon that would fire steel ball bearings. Plus a few pipe bombs! If kids did that today they'd go straight to jail and they would throw away the key. Anyway, Bobby and I got quite an education in chemistry, what between Jack and our Barrett cousins.

Once we got back to Salt Lake, we asked Jack about how we could go about making some cracker balls ourselves. Jack said, "No problem. I know how to make some out of red phosphorus, potassium chlorate, powered magnesium, sulfur and powdered charcoal. We can buy all that stuff at the chemical plant in Salt Lake. There is just one thing though, you have to mix it wet or it can blow up on you, and it's strong enough to take off body parts." Quite a jump from our little cracker balls—that we knew. "If I make this for you," said Jack, "Don't tell Mom and Dad or they'll kill me, and you boys, too."

So to the chemical plant we go. At that time you could get just about any chemical you wanted, if you were over twenty-one, and Jack was. When we got back home, we went down into the basement and Jack started making us a cracker ball. Mother and Dad thought we were playing with the chemistry set they gave us for Christmas. After it was all mixed up, Jack rolled the red clay-like mixture up in a piece of paper. It looked like a big red snow cone. I couldn't wait to go fire it off, but Jack said we would have to let it dry first. A few hours passed, and our cracker ball was dry, so Bobby, Jack and I took our monster cracker ball to outside the city limits. We got out of the car, and I asked Jack how we were gonna shoot it off with no fuse. Jack grinned and at the same time tossed underhanded our cracker ball about twenty-five feet and hollered get down. I never heard such a BOOM! A cloud of smoke went up like an atomic bomb and when the smoke cleared, there was a three foot hole left in the ground. Bobby said, "Jack, I don't think we can throw those cracker balls at each other!" We all couldn't stop laughing. What a gut buster. We only had one bomb so we went home and decided the day was shot and we would make another one the next day.

The next morning, after a great bacon, eggs, biscuits, and cream gravy breakfast that my mother could make like no other, we headed for the basement to our secret lab to mix up another cracker ball. After Jack finished, he said, "I'm a little tired. I need to catch up on my sleep, so I'm gonna go up to my room and take a nap. But first I'm laying this bomb up here on the furnace while it dries. Don't touch it!" His room was the guest room upstairs just above the furnace.

Bobby and I were into flying model airplanes out in the back lot so that is what we decided to do while Jack took his nap. I fired up my little thimble drome biplane and round and round it went. After a couple of hours and a hundred or so laps, I was coming around and could see over the fence that the top of the house a great blue white cloud of smoke that resembled the atomic bomb cloud. Then it dawned on Bobby and I, that the cracker ball on the furnace had somehow had exploded. Bobby and I ran like a skunked bird dog to the back of the house and noticed immediately that all the windows around the basement were no longer there.

We could hear Dad down the staircase calling our names as if he thought we were blown to bits. When he came up and saw that we were all right, he started yelling, "Thank God! Thank God! Y'all are all right!" About that time, here comes the fire department and all the neighbors from all around, and then Dad became a whole different person. He said, "I should have never bought you boys that chemistry set for Christmas. I just learned a good lesson. I hope you boys did also. If y'all had been in the basement, you would have been killed." Jack made his way to where we were. Dad was lecturing us and he was white as a ghost. When the bomb went off it woke him out of a deep sleep and he said it raised him up a couple of feet off his bed. Bobby and I didn't tell Dad that Jack made the bomb. It would have caused a lot of trouble between Mom and Dad. Thank God, we only took enough of the chemicals to make one bomb in the basement at a time. The rest Jack had hid in the garage, so even the fire department thought it was the chemistry set. I guess all the excitement and stress of the thought of Dad finding out was too much for Jack, and he went back to work a day earlier than expected.

After a few days, the house was repaired, and things started getting back to normal. Bobby and me got the old cracker ball bug again. We just didn't know when to quit. The stuff was still in the garage, and Bobby said, "Let's try to make some like Jack made, only smaller so they'll be like the real cracker balls we had on the Fourth." He said he didn't remember how to make the mixture and asked me if I did. I said, "Yes!" My big chance to prove myself as good as Bobby. Mother had to go to the store and Dad was still at work, which gave us the opportunity to make it. So very cautiously, Bobby and I went and retrieved the chemicals from the garage and brought them down to the basement.

I got a pail of water to mix it wet like Jack had said, and was doing just fine, but I was spilling a little powder of one chemical here and a little of another chemical there and while I was mixing the wet stuff, the stuff that was dry on the table some way got all mixed together and ignited with one big flash. It didn't blow up, thank God, but it did ignite the wet stuff also. In the process it burned my middle finger real bad. Somehow we got the fire out before anyone found out. But the worst wasn't over yet. Bobby said, "I think I read in the old chemistry book that a red phosphorus burn was deadly if it got into the blood stream." He found the manual, which wasn't destroyed when the first bomb blew. Sure enough, that's what it said. Mother came home from the store, but I just couldn't bring myself to tell her. Then Dad came home from work, but he had to leave right away to go to Pinedale, Wyoming because an oil well was having trouble. You talk about sweating it out and afraid to say anything because of almost blowing up the house again and thinking I was going to die at the same time. Later on that night I just couldn't take it anymore. I finally broke down and confessed to Mother. She just couldn't believe it.

She said, "My God, what in the world would make a sane person do something like that?" My mother was very understanding, so we confessed the whole story, even about Jack's part. She said, "This is one incident I don't ever want your dad to find out about." Then she got me to the hospital emergency room. The burn hadn't broken the skin, so no poison got in my blood stream—I'm still kicking!!!!

Life really started picking up in Salt Lake at that time. We were living the good life. Dad was making good money and we bought a boat. We went to Half Moon Lake, close to Pinedale, Wyoming and learned to water ski. The lakes were unspoiled, unlike today.

Early that spring—there was still snow on the ground—Bobby and I decided to water ski behind this really nice inboard that a fellow worker of Dad's had. It was extremely fast. My Dad's friend said, It's okay to ski, but whatever you do don't fall off, 'cause the water is still close to freezing." That didn't scare us. We had learned to ski pretty damn good, but not over

LEFT: *Jack Leflar*; CENTER: *Joyce Fuller*;
RIGHT: *Randy and Bobby*

about thirty-five MPH. I put on a slalom. Bobby put on two skis and off we went. Dad's friend had been drinking pretty heavy, and Dad had enjoyed a couple of beers. They got to talking and were not keeping a eye on Bob and me. The boat started going faster and faster until it reached about sixty mph. Dad turned around and took one look at me frozen with fear, and made his friend slow down and take us in. I decided to go fishing instead. There were a lot of native trout still around and that sounded a lot better than sixty MPH on a frozen lake!

Now and then Dad would take us up to Pinedale, Wyoming, where they were putting up a new well. It was really something to see, and it was in the most remote wilderness part of Wyoming. Sometimes there would be a small stream running near the well, just full of six inch native brook trout. They were so hungry you could catch them on a bare hook. And we'd hunt sage chickens—you had to get the young ones because the older ones had way too much of a sage taste.

One time I went out with Dad to an oil rig that was on fire, and one of Dad's friends got burned real bad. I heard him ask Dad, "Take my ring off, Lassies, and give it too my wife." Then he died. 'Lassies' was the nickname the roughnecks gave to Dad. Every time they would go in to town on the days off and order breakfast, Dad would always say; "Pass the Lassies", for "molasses". The well was burning out of control and they needed to close a valve, but it was too hot to get at. Dad got the idea that if he could shoot the valve with his 300 Magnum with a scope, he could turn it with several shots. It was a success. My pop was the man of the day. Usually they would call in the well known Red Adair to put out an oil field fire—that guy ended up working up through Kuwait and the Gulf War.

Bobby and I and mother got to watch when, as they say in the oil business, "the well's come in." That's when they hit a

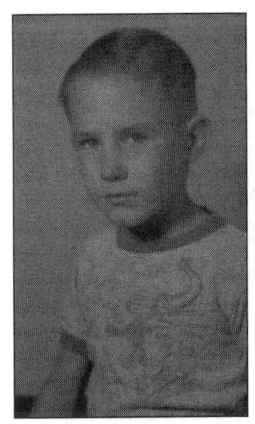

LEFT: *Bobby;* CENTER TOP: *Lawson with the boys;*
CENTER BOTTOM: *Randy;* RIGHT: *Jack Leflar*

pocket of gas or oil, and it blows way up in the sky. It is quite a sight. The roughnecks would have to work hard and fast, with oil raining on them, to cap the well and install a shut off valve. It was very dangerous work.

One day in 1957, Dad came home from work, with a look on his face you didn't see much on a man that loved life, and sadly said to mother, "Well Loraine, the gas company wants to transfer me to an office job with the big shots, with a raise—to El Paso. Mother said, "Oh no! Not El Paso," and she started crying. Bobby said, "Dad, I can't leave my music and my friends and school." Bobby had just started Evergreen Junior High School and had fallen in love with the school's music program. I didn't want to leave either. I had a lot of pet birds—bantam chickens, quail and pheasants, and a flock of special bred pigeons-- Modenas, Tumblers, White Kings. My favorite was a little bantam rooster that had long spurs and was the champion chicken fighter of the neighborhood. Mother had very personal reasons for not wanting to go to El Paso—she had too many painful memories about life with Tommy Leflar.

After all the negative emotional outbreaks, we all knew

that the move would be best for the family, since Dad would be getting a lot better income. It would also be easier on him to have an office job, as he was reaching his sixties.

CHAPTER TWO

COOL IT!

The city of El Paso is insulated by miles of desert
east and west, with a mountain range to the north and
the Rio Grande river and Mexico to the south. Fifty years ago,
the city was a melting pot in a vacuum, an incubator ready to blow,
with its natural boundaries keeping what was going on in town, in,
while outside influences flowed in fast and furious.

"I was going on thirteen, and Bobby was fourteen, on the day we pulled into El Paso," says Randy. "My God, what a let down. Nothing but dry heat and bright sun and sand dunes. To Bobby and me, it was the next thing to hell after living in Farmington and Salt Lake, with all their beautiful mountains, trees, rivers and streams. There are mountains in and around El Paso but they are very rugged and desolate. My parents rented a house on Honeysuckle Drive between Montana and Cielo Vista Drive. To the left of the new house was the desert area where Biggs Air Force and Fort Bliss Military did their training. To the north was all desert, mostly open range ranch land, full of rattlesnakes, jackrabbits, cottontails, coyotes, ground squirrels and lots of horned toads, lizards, red tail hawks, antelope, bobcats and deer, doves and quail. Most of the wildlife you would never see in the daytime, they seemed to all be in hiding

David Welty on the drums and Johnny Daniels and Bob Fuller on guitars demonstrate their talents while trying out for the annual P-TA Variety Show, which is to be held March 31 in the Auditorium.

until the sun went down. Bobby and I started school at Burges High School, to begin the same process just like we did before when we moved from Farmington to Salt Lake—trying to fit in. This time, it was hard for me. My grades rapidly declined. Of course Bobby once again became one of the most popular students and was put in the senior band right away. Whereas poor little me got put in the junior band. Not because of being a bad trombone player, as I had gotten pretty darn good by this time. I think it was because of being younger. I did make first chair though. Hey, look at me!"

Randy may have felt he was inferior in scholastics, but for his brother, school was truly running a serious distant second to rock and roll by this time. Bobby's grades had been on a steep decline back in Salt Lake City where his last report card shows near-failing grades at the end of ninth grade, where he had begun the year as an A/B student. In fact, he had never been much of a student, barely keeping his grades above sea level, as is evidenced by his bizarre spellings of common words in many of his handwritten notes. Regardless, as a newcomer at Burges, it did not take long for Bobby to impress the kids. A school drum battle is recalled where a few big shots were trying to out drum each other, and Bobby was begging for a chance—much to their amusement. When they finally handed him the sticks, he stomped over the other guys in a demonstration of power and confidence. Bobby would soon gain a reputation as one of the hottest drummers in town.

Another move came for the Fullers in 1958. "My dad had a house built about three miles away, in a new subdivision called Eastwood," relates Randy. "The address of the new house was 9509 Album Avenue. Kind of a weird address for musicians, wouldn't you think? Coincidence or fate? You tell me!" The boys were faced again with fitting into new schools and new friendships. Now bona fide teenagers, they still couldn't quite pack away their wild west younger days.

Sterling Brooks was a local kid who lived around the corner and down the street on Rutherglen in the neighboring Scottsdale subdivision. He recalls, "Mr. Fuller and my dad both worked for El Paso Natural Gas Company. Scottsdale was close to the airport where my dad worked, and where many El Paso Natural Gas Company employees lived. It seemed like we socialized almost exclusively with other EPNG families. When my folks would go visit the Fullers, I would tag along so that I would get to hang out with the guys at their house. Mostly, we hung out in the backyard and the garage, where Bobby and Randy had a pet squirrel in a cage. Bobby had some parts from his Soap Box Derby car there, in addition to their guitars and amplifiers. Being nine years younger than Bobby, almost to the day—our birthdays were in October—I was too young to really be interested in the musical instruments. The squirrel was the most fascinating diversion in the garage. It nearly bit the end of my finger off one day, and I stayed away from the cage after that. One day, Bobby gave me his blue plastic Soap Box Derby helmet. He raced a car that he had built in the garage. The races back then were in northeast El Paso off a street that intersected Dyer Street and ran east and west. The street sloped away from the Franklin Mountains and had the perfect grade for racing these little cars that ran on gravity. My dad and I went to the race that Bobby was in. It was a Saturday morning and I recall the weather was perfect. At the time, Bobby didn't have any fans, as he hadn't become famous yet. It was pretty much just me, my dad and Mr. Fuller hollering for Bobby as he blasted down the street in his Soap Box Derby car. If memory serves me right, Bobby didn't come in first, second or even third in his class, and I suspect he lost interest in Soap Box Derby racing after that. I guess he tossed in the towel, and that's why he gave me his blue plastic helmet. I suspect that by then, he was more interested in the guitars, amplifiers and drums that they had stowed in the garage."

"When we moved," says Randy, "they made Bob and me

LEFT: *Randy*; RIGHT: *Teenage hijinx*

I FOUGHT THE LAW

These are the winners of the P-TA Talent Show held March 31, 1960 in the J. M. Hanks Auditorium. Singing is Bob Fyller; on the drums, is David Welty; and on the guitar, Johnny Daniel. The winner was chosen by applause. Photo by Dennis Barrett

transfer to Bel Air High, a new school without much tradition like the older schools we were used to, and we were not very happy there. Especially Bobby. For one thing, the school band was terrible and he was used to the best. He did, however, become very popular again in no time. The girls really liked him. They were always hanging around him in the halls between classes. That's when Bobby and I started in some ways to drift apart. I never did figure it out but either he was embarrassed of me or just downright jealous of his little brother. I was so much better looking! No, seriously, I had become angry and more insecure. I guess you might say

I was kind of a hothead ready for a fight. Who wanted to be around a brother like that? He told me one time that I was getting to be a lot like Jack. I said, 'Thanks for the compliment.' I looked up to Jack."

"I tried to go out for track and football, but you had get above a C average to play and mine was up and down. I didn't like Bel Air. Sports were a big thing for me and now suddenly, we move and I'm not allowed to play anything. When we were younger, back in Salt Lake, we pole vaulted and high jumped, ran track and long jumped. Then, in El Paso, things changed and I couldn't keep the grade average," rues Randy. "I couldn't play sports, so I joined a bunch of other hotheads called the Tartarus Association," he adds, "You know, from Greek mythology. Our motto was *From The Depths Of Hell*. It was Jimmy Wagnon, Tinker Wiecke, Ted Braithwaite and me, and some other guys from Bel Air. We'd race around in these scooters that were really fast. Loud mufflers. We said that we were a good Samaritan gang, but actually we were just a bunch of thugs wanting to kick ass, you know. We'd wear white bucks with horseshoe taps on the back and we'd clomp down the halls at school like we were Jerry Lee Lewis or somebody. Our names were on the back of our white jacket. The lettering looked like graffiti before its time. They went for it at school, 'Oh, you guys can do this, sure,' like it was a fraternity or something, but it turned out to be like we were kicking peoples' asses, like being our own kind of Robin Hood types. We prowled the neighborhood on our scooters. We were helping people *not* get their ass kicked, by kicking other peoples' asses. We turned out being more like Jesse James and less like Robin Hood. The bullies got their asses whooped by other bullies—that was us, the other ones."

One reason Bobby was not in the Tartarus Association

was that he had successfully bailed out of Bel Air High School, handing in greener pastures at Ysleta HS. Randy recalls, "Bobby talked Mom and Dad into letting him transfer to an older school in the Lower Valley, one with a lot of tradition, with the best band and sports program of any school around—Ysleta High. He became drum major there, and assistant band director, taking over the class when the instructor was sick or on vacation. After he left Bel Air, I started to become depressed because it seemed as though I wouldn't achieve any success in any courses other than Band and Physical Education. Mother and Dad began to worry about me. They tried to help me with my grades, but they just seemed to make things worse. You know, the competition game between Bobby and I. They meant well, but I was just too far gone."

"I really looked up to my brother Jack," says Randy. "Right around this time with my school problem, he came to visit again, but this time he had a broken leg. He said he had been moving a three hundred pound drill pipe around with a little roughneck fella they called Shorty, when the little guy had dropped his end and the pipe hit the ground so hard that it knocked it out of Jack's hands, hit his leg and fractured it. He had to wear a cast for a while. Dad let him stay with us until he could work again. There always seemed to be some stress between them. Jack wasn't his son. He was Mother's boy. I liked Jack and it was good to have him around. One time, when Jack was back on his feet, my Uncle Holbert and Aunt Mattie, with my favorite cousin Don, all on the Fuller side, came to visit. Bobby had a date that night, so Jack and I decided to show Don the town. I was fifteen at the time, Jack twenty-nine, and Don was eighteen. Mom and Dad were talking in the living room with my uncle and aunt, when we started out the door. My dad said, 'Whoa, boys, where do you think you're going?' I said,

I FOUGHT THE LAW

LEFT: *Randy, grad;*
RIGHT: *Bobby*

'We're just going up to the Oasis,' I said, meaning a popular drive-in restaurant where teenagers and young adults used to hang out, 'to cruise the drive-ins and check the hotrods and girls out.' He said, 'Okay, but don't get in trouble.' And Uncle Holbert said, in a very firm tone, 'And stay away from Juarez, Mexico. Especially you Don!' Well they should of never mentioned Juarez, because that's the first place we went, and boy was that a mistake. All the way over, Jack kept saying, 'Yeah, Don! Tonight's the night, I'm gonna show my little brother how to be a man!' When we reached Juarez, we stopped in a night club called the Lobby, a popular place where Long John Hunter, a well known funky blues musician performed. We drank a few Dos Equis Mexican beers and then started hitting club after club until we were all drunk. Hey, beer was a nickel! The last joint we came to was way back off the main strip. It was an old building that looked like it could have been an old Mexican jailhouse in the Pancho Villa days. We were the only Caucasians in the place. We sat down on three stools, Don on the left, Jack in the middle and me on the right, and Jack ordered three more Dos Equis. I said, 'Jack, I can't drink no more' and proceeded to throw up in a trough, just under the bar by our feet. 'Go ahead little brother, heave it all up and have anoth-

I FOUGHT THE LAW

er drink like a man,' he laughed. Well, this big Mexican dude was sitting to the right of me, and made a wisecrack how I was just a little gringo pussy, and Jack responded with, 'He may be a pussy, but my little brother can lick any Mexican in here.' Jack should of never said that, because when I came up from puking, I said, 'Yeah, I can,' and gave him a right hook to the jaw. Jack and Don were talking to someone else and didn't see me hit the dude. The Mexican said, 'You piece of shit gringo,' and grabbed me by the throat, and starting choking me. All the time I'm trying to get Jack and Don's attention, but could barely whisper. All of a sudden Jack turned around, saw what was going on, and popped the Mexican in the nose. It lifted him up off the stool and he slid across the room on the floor, unconscious. Wow! What a punch!"

"About that time the whole bar jumped on us," continues Randy. "There were fists flying everywhere. Finally Jack caught one in the mouth, but no one noticed because by that time the drunks were fighting amongst each other. Don and I, in all the ruckus, got Jack and made our way outside and down the street. We were just about a block from the checkpoint, walking along with our arms around each other, laughing and bragging how we showed them who's boss. Then Jack said, 'I told you Randell, I was gonna show you how to be a man to-

LEFT: *Long John Hunter*; RIGHT: *The Lobby, Juarez*

night.' About that time this little plainclothes Federale came up to us and started yelling, 'Why'd you start that fight, you fucking gringos?' Jack said, 'Oh man, just leave us alone, were sorry, we just want to go home. My lip's torn, and I need to get it stitched up.' Well that little Federale just wouldn't shut up, so Jack popped him one and knocked him into a parked car, and slowly the little cop slid down and laid out against the tire. Then he suddenly came to and grabbed a whistle from his pocket, and started blowing it as loud as he could. Out of nowhere came one Federale after another. Jack said, 'Don, you and Randell get the hell outta here. Try to make the border while I hold them off.' Thank God, Don and I made it. The last thing I remember was turning around while we were running, and seeing Jack fighting with ten or more Federales until he went down. I felt so bad at the time, and very proud of the sacrifice he had made for us. Don and I walked in the front door to face the music. Soon as we went in, Dad was still up with Uncle Holbert. The first thing he said was, 'You boys went to Juarez, didn't you?' We said yes. Then Dad said, 'Where's Jack?' I sadly said, 'He's in jail in Juarez.'

  Randy was glad that summer had come at last. "I started running around with one of my best friends who I had met at Burges High, good old Jimmy Wagnon. Jimmy and I did a lot of hunting together in the desert. He was from Mississippi and loved to talk about the Civil War. Plus, he was a damn good artist. He loved to draw pictures of soldiers in combat, and he kept on trying to talk me into going to military school our sophomore year. I told him my grades were not good enough. Jimmy said, 'That's okay. I hear that it being a private school, they really help you and sometimes they pass you anyway.' That sounded really good to me. It meant maybe I could play football. Actually that was my dream, but you had to make your

I FOUGHT THE LAW

LEFT: *Bobby, 1956*; RIGHT: *Randy, cadet*

grades at Bel Air or you sat on the bench. That's what I did. I think I could have been good enough in those days to maybe play college and even go pro—if I ever made my grades. After a couple of weeks, Jimmy talked me into asking my folks if I could go to Allen Military School in Bryan, Texas. I was shocked—they thought it was a fantastic idea. So, I decided to go. Anything, I thought, would be better than Bel Air High. We still had a lot of summer left and with the vision of playing the guitar and singing like Elvis, I bought me a Gretsch Country Gentleman guitar and started learning how to play. It finally looked like I was going to be able to play an instrument that would get me a bit more attention than my brother. If that was at all possible! Jimmy bought a set a drums and we practiced a little during vacation, and we got pretty good. We learned a few songs, mostly Jimmy Reed and Bo Diddley and just got to jamming. Bobby got a job at the Kurland-Salzman Music store in downtown El Paso, and started meeting a lot of influential people, such as DJ's and other musicians that played around town."

"Then it was time to end the fun of the free life and pack up and get down to good old Allen Military School, says Randy. "Dad and I left and drove down together. It was a long drive, almost 700 miles across the state of Texas. I was excited about

I FOUGHT THE LAW

going and couldn't wait to get there. Jimmy and his folks had left a day earlier. I was glad that he broke the ice first. Jimmy had another El Paso friend at Allen, named Russell Plyler. He was the one who had talked Jimmy into going there. When Dad and I arrived, Jimmy and Russell met me at the commandant's office to register, and Jimmy mentioned to me that yet another one of our friends had decided to come. Tommy Breen was another troubled kid who needed some discipline. So there were four guys from El Paso that we all knew of. After we registered, we got our uniforms and checked into our dormitories. Our folks left, so we decided to stroll over to the mess hall and get something to eat. Since it was the first day, we didn't have to worry about military procedures, but there were a few hard asses with rank that just had to play the role. We got in line at the mess hall, Russell first, me second, Jimmy last, and went through the food chain, and Russell went to sit down first at a table with some other boys already in uniform. Russell was a second lieutenant, and a real nice guy. Then I set down next to Russell and Jimmy next to me, when this lieutenant looked me straight in the eye and said, 'This is for commissioned officers only, so leave!' Well, being the type to take no shit off of no one I said, 'I don't see any signs.' Russell poked me in the side and softly said, 'Cool it!' Then the lieutenant said, 'You are a smart ass aren't you? Where are you from?' 'I am from El Paso, Your Honor, and at least I'm not a asshole like you.' I want you to know that this pissed that junior college lieutenant OFF. He said, 'I'll be waiting for you behind the mess hall and I'm going teach you some manners.' I said, 'I'll be there!'" Then he got up and left. Russell said, 'Randell, you just made a big mistake. Your first day here you'll get demerits, and you will get your your ass kicked because he's one of the toughest guys at school. He can really fight.' Jimmy said, 'Randell can handle himself, I saw him kick the heck out of a guy during vacation.' By the time we got through eating, the whole school knew about the fight and I overheard how everyone said I was going to get my ass kicked. I almost backed down because he was so much older, but then the whole school would look at me as a coward, and I couldn't live with that on top of all my other insecurity problems. Out to the back we go!"

"Slowly," adds Randy, "Jimmy, Russell and I made our way to the back of the mess hall and all the time I'm thinking, what did I get myself into? As we came around the corner, the whole school was there to watch the fight. Well, to make a long story short, I beat him fair and square, and I became really good friends with that lieutenant. I also won the respect of most of the recruits. Jimmy and I both joined the marching band. We both were probably the two best musicians Allen Academy had, especially in the drum and trombone section. We put a little Dixieland band together with two other musicians, Bobby Gross on clarinet and piano, and Tom Daly on tuba. Everyone liked us so much that they let us play for all the basketball games, even when they went out of town. On the band break, Jimmy and I would play the guitar and drums. Jimmy would sing *I'm a Grass Snake* and *Little Red Rooster*. The audience loved it. We played a lot in Louisiana where blues was popular. The marching band got to play for the Mardi Gras parade. I saw the Everly Brothers in the parade singing Claudette on a flatbed truck. And that really made me want to be a rock and roller instead of a football player. Anyway, there were some mighty big farm boys and Cajuns on the football team and I didn't want to break my extremely talented fingers. It was getting to be Christmas time and Dad got one of the company planes to fly Jimmy and me to El Paso over the holidays. We hadn't been home since we started school and we were looking forward to seeing our families and friends. I brought along my guitar, thinking I might show Bobby a lick or two. To my surprise, Bobby had not only also started playing the guitar, but he already had his own band and had won a talent contest to boot. He was recording on an Ampex two-track that he'd bought with the money he made from the music store. Once again, Everybody Loves Bobby. What a disaster. Would I ever overcome this sibling rivalry, of being second best to my brother? I felt so jealous and lost. Here I was at this military school that I didn't really care for and meanwhile, here's Bobby back home getting all the girls and perfecting the same dream that I wanted. Whoa! Blaze."

"Suddenly, I didn't want to go back to Allen Academy," Randy recalls. "I begged and pleaded with Dad to let me stay home so I could at least play guitar with Bob. Dad really got upset and explained about how much money he would lose, and how I needed to get my grades. He darn near started crying, so I agreed to go back. I never saw Dad cry before and I didn't want to be the first one to make him. Jimmy Wagnon and I flew back to Allen after the holidays and started our routine of classes and learning to be pre-soldiers for Texas A&M or the real Army. That was what most of the students went to Allen Academy for, to make a career out of the service. I guess us El Paso Boys were of a different breed because most of the time we were in trouble, marching off demerits double-time. I think I had a few hundred because of going AWOL with Bobby Gross. He talked me into to hitchhiking to his hometown in Groom, Texas about four hundred miles from Bryan. We didn't have any clothes except the uniforms we had on and no money. Bobby Gross made it sound so good, I couldn't resist. He said we could hitch a ride easy, 'cause people would think we were in the service. In Groom, Bobby's mother owned the only motel in town and he said we could have our own room, and go hunting and fishing all day. How could anyone turn that down? When Dad found out we had gone AWOL, he had another company plane that was in that area pick us up and take us back to Hell. Excuse me, I mean Allen Academy. Well, we got through the term and finally, it was June. Oh, happy day! Military school had come to an end. I could hardly wait to get home to El Paso. That old desert was sure going to look good. I was really happy, in a way shocked, that I would be a junior in high school with above average grades. And I knew Mom and Dad were proud of the fact that I saw it through to the end."

CHAPTER THREE

THUNDER

El Paso County is the furthest west point in the state of Texas, closer to California than it is to Houston, and in a totally different time zone from the rest of the state. It is a world unto itself, and its denizens have always known that.

While Randy had been tucked away at military school on the other side of the state, Bobby had begun playing drums in a band with Jim Reese, who would become an integral part of the Bobby Fuller story, as well as being a vital part of the 1950s and early 1960s El Paso rock and roll scene, before Bobby's climb to fame.

Jim played in the legendary Counts of *Thunder* fame, which featured the incredible Bobby Taylor. The guitar was his calling, but he played piano with the Counts. Jim recalled, "In the mid 50's, before the Counts, really, there were only two bands in town, the Rock Kings and the Rhythm Heirs. When the Rock Kings lost their guitar player, they approached me about filling the position. I was so excited about finally playing with some other people and was ready to go over to audition when like ten minutes before I was going to leave the house they called me up and said never mind, they'd found someone else. I was devastated! A couple of months later, I was walking down the street and two guys pull over in a car, and like one of them was Bobby Taylor, known to be a local tough, so I thought, man, I've HAD it! You had to know Bobby back then. He had long hair way before it was fashionable and when he and Willie Wilson, his drummer, pulled up like that to me and I really thought they were gonna whoop on me, but what they ended up wanting to know was, would I play piano because they needed a piano player in their band and I said, 'oh yeah, I can play the piano'—although all I'd really ever done was thump along on the old out of tune thing at home. 'YEAH! YOU BET I CAN PLAY PIANO!' So I went right home and started learning to play that thing! That was the start of the Counts, really. Bobby (Taylor) played lead guitar, I played piano, Willie Wilson played drums and we had Bobby's brother Glen on acoustic rhythm guitar. We didn't have a bass player because I'd play the bass lines on the piano."

Not long after their formation, the band cut two of the all-time coolest instrumentals in recorded history, *Thunder* and *Taylor's Rock*, which were recorded at radio station KALG in Alamogordo, New Mexico. Alamogordo was also home to Yucca Records, the studio and record label that released the 45 RPM single for the band in 1958. Jim recalls the session, "During the recording of *Thunder*, we would all yell stuff during the four bar drum solo. The yell that stands out is Willie Wilson, the drummer, shouting, 'Oh, little bit!' That's how he got the name, Little Bit."

Thunder is primitive, pounding, commanding—the definitive Southwest rock and roll instrumental, and a yardstick against which all recordings of the time should be measured, from the booming thrash of the tom-toms barreling up against a wild guitar and steady piano-pounding from Jim Reese, who at the age of sixteen was both beginning and ending a career

I FOUGHT THE LAW

LEFT: *Bobby, Jim Reese, Dalton Powell 1962*

on the ivories. Although the tiny custom 45 RPM pressing, as Yucca 102, which lists only Bobby Taylor (not the Counts) on the label, didn't skyrocket to the top of the charts, it did well locally. It should, however, have been a nationwide hit.

According to Calvin Boles, George Goldner, who was in the process of selling his interest in Roulette Records to Morris Levy, had assured him of sales of 100,000 copies if 'they' took over distribution. Boles said he was thrilled about the idea of making the big time, but no contract ever did arrive, and after several weeks, it became apparent to him that they had stalled just to keep *Thunder* from competing with the remarkably similar Duane Eddy offering *Ramrod*, which shows Al Casey as the songwriter on the label, but which actually lists Morris Levy as a co-writer! At the end of the day, Dick Clark's boy Duane hit #27 on the Billboard Hot 100 chart, while the brilliant Bob Taylor record would remain an obscure gem.

The instrumental foursome soon expanded to include not one, but two dueling vocalists, Jerry Bright and Morris 'Googie' Dirmeyer, and occasionally Mike Shockley came in to play upright bass. Jim recalls also doing his share of singing, "I sang on the big piano numbers, stuff by Fats Domino, Jerry Lee Lewis, Little Richard, Larry Williams, Huey Smith and also some Elvis. I can remember playing some gigs and girls hanging around all over the piano, but I was too naive and ignorant to know what to do. It was a long time before I experienced The Big Thrill."

Another type of Big Thrill did come when Bobby Taylor asked Jim to play rhythm guitar on the second Counts 45, which Jim recalls as being financed by a sax player he remembers only as Johnny. "He was a carpenter or a housepainter, I think," says Jim. "I don't remember who's on the piano or that really rough bass, but that is Willie Wilson on drums. *Child of Fortune* and *Don't Be Unfair* were cut, if I remember correctly, at a makeshift studio in El Paso that had all these crazy grey paper egg cartons nailed all over the walls for acoustics."

Although Bobby Taylor didn't sing when the band played live, his vocal performance on these two songs is stunning. The A-side, *Child of Fortune* is so deliberately slow that it sounds like it's playing at the wrong speed, but the taunt and threat of the beat backs a raw and wild, agonized, tortured tale of woe. The sax man, known only as Johnny, moans along like an ailing duck—a fantastic ailing duck, one might add. This chilling lament, for all of its perfect pain and anguish, is coupled with the frantic *Don't Be Unfair*, hyped up, pure rock and roll bulging with big, booming drums, frantic, gulping vocals, drunken sax and echo-soaked guitar. This is, indisputably, one of the most sensational rockers set to plastic, and here, it's the

I FOUGHT THE LAW

B-side, even.

The Counts played all of the local teen spots, from bowling alleys to school dances, but the high point of their career was landing a regular gig with the city parks department, which provided the band with a flatbed truck and power hookups, so they could set up at different local shopping centers each week. Recalls Jim, "Back then, El Paso had a real problem with kids running wild in the streets and stuff, so the city supplied us with a flatbed truck and power to run our equipment and we'd just pass the hat. It kept the city happy 'cause the kids were all in one place, not running crazy in the streets, causing grief. These shopping center shows got pretty wild! One time we played and police estimated we had three thousand kids dancing in the parking lot! Really, we were the only real rock and roll band in town. I mean the Rhythm Heirs were big but they were more of a Mexican soul band, and there was also the Rock Kings but they were more soul influenced, too. Then there was us, the Counts. I've always called the Counts a pure rock and roll band. A rock and roll garage band. We just grabbed our guitars and drums and beat on 'em. The louder, the better! No tremendous amount of finesse, but the kids didn't seem to care. Neither did we! A typical Counts show was one wild, no-holds-barred rock and roll brawl. I've never experienced such raw, brute, emotion-packed music in my life! To me, that's what rock and roll should be, and hasn't been since 1958. You know, the Counts were denounced from several El Paso pulpits as 'tools of the devil,' and I can sort of see why. We really put on a show. You know, Bobby Taylor never moved at all. He just sat hunched on his amp, with his greasy hair hanging all over his face, mean and tough looking as all hell. Our singers, Jerry and Googie, were somewhat of a novelty, as back then most everybody played an instrument, even the singer. They kept the energy going, jumping around and getting the kids crazy."

"The only reason I left the Counts," Jim explained, "was that I wanted to play guitar all the time. There were some internal problems toward the end and the band actually split in two, with both halves asking me to go with them. I asked which half would have me as a guitar player and the half that said okay got me, and we became the Royal Lancers. If I could've played guitar with the Counts, though, I would have stayed with them. Anyway, the Royal Lancers had a lot going for them at the time and we were unique, because we had two drummers, but one at a time. I guess you'd call them co-drummers. Jerry Bright and Googie Dirmeyer each sang and played the drums, and when one'd sing, the other'd play, and vice versa."

Howard Steele was a rock and roll teenager, about to dive into the wild band scene. "The real reason that the Counts broke up is that Willie Wilson, the drummer, and somebody else in the band, stole a case of beer off a beer truck, and they had the choice of joining the Army or going to jail. They joined the Army and that fractured the band and then the next version of that was the Royal Lancers. Maybe Jim didn't remember that, but that's what happened. I first saw the Royal Lancers in 1958 and I thought they were great. The band was Jim Reese on guitar, and Dalton Powell, was the piano player, and Jerry Bright and Googie Dirmeyer on drums, and there was a bass player Mike Ciccarelli, who couldn't play with them all the time. I was in the same classes in school as Jim at McLaughlin Junior High, so one day, I talked to him. I said, 'Jim, I want to be in the band. Can I play percussion or something?' And he says, 'Why don't you get a bass?' See their bass player, Mike, worked for the railroad, so he couldn't make all the gigs. So I went home and said to Dad, 'I need a bass,' and he said, 'Okay,' and he took me to the music store where he told me,

'The payments for the bass are sixteen dollars a month, and you pay them or the bass goes back.' And then I went back to Jim and said, 'Okay Jim, I got the bass,' and Jim showed me how to play it some. I really have to credit him for my whole musical career, because that's really where I got my start, with Jim Reese. I got my first recording job working at KHEY radio station here. I was a staff engineer, and on the holidays, Christmas and New Years, the chief engineer would send me out with these great professional microphones and tape recorders to record the local UTEP (University of Texas at El Paso) chorus and their orchestra, plus all the Christmas pageants at all the high schools, so we could play those tapes on the radio over Christmas and New Years so that the jocks could have time off. Those were the first recording things I ever did. And then, you know, we dabbled at the house with the equipment. We'd record on a little tape recorder and I'd go to the radio station and bump it up to full blast on tapes so that records could be pressed."

"We ended up playing together as the Royal Lancers for almost two years," said Jim, "and then we changed our name to the Embers, after a night club I'd seen that summer in McAllen, Texas. At first, the Embers line up was Jerry Bright on vocals, Dalton Powell on piano, me on lead guitar, Sonny Fletcher on rhythm guitar, and Howard Steele on bass. We had a drummer but we really wanted to replace him. That's when we got Bobby Fuller."

As early as 1959 and into 1960, three fourths of the future Bobby Fuller Four—Bobby, Jim, and Dalton—were making noise in a band together, although in a very different formation.

CHAPTER FOUR

JUAREZ

The Lobby, it was a pit. It was a mangy pit where money could buy you anything you wanted, but the clientele was sound and the place was notorious. If you went in there, you were going to get something that was way beyond rock and roll.

Mike Ciccarelli speaks of the Lobby in hallowed tones, "You know, here was Mexico, which was totally decadent and anything goes, money buys anything, and it's like incredible. God, I was goin' over there by the time I was sixteen years old. You'd get a hard-on for twenty-five cents. The reason we went over there was to see Little Joe Washington or Long John Hunter at the Lobby. The Lobby was the place. That's where I think Bobby got some energy. He understood what was happening at the Lobby. That was incorporated into the music because it was blazing. They'd get over there and could have anything they wanted, they were making money like they'd never seen in a cotton field or a box factory. They were getting booze, drugs, cars, anything they wanted. If they wanted to get shuttled back to the American side, they could, etc. So they rolled out the red carpet for these guys and what they got in return was some of the most blazing stuff, this side of Hendrix. You could not bring cameras into the Lobby. It was forbidden and if you had a camera in there, they would pull you and the camera out, or if they had a night when they had really tough bouncers there, they'd take the camera away, or take the film out and keep it. This was done to protect the clientele. Because there was so much graft, who knows if they were going to get the chief of police or this or that, I don't know. They want to be guaranteed anonymity, of course. So you risked your life unless you figured how to get a picture in there without a flash. Nobody got anything of Long John, they covered him. When he played, when they were cranking, they had a two hundred pound bouncer in front of the bandstand at all times. There is only one picture of him in existence at the Lobby, in his early thirties. You could get your ass kicked hard for taking a picture. The Lobby, it was a pit. It was a mangy pit where money could buy anything you wanted, but the clientele was sound and the place was notorious. If you went in there, you were going to get something that was way beyond rock and roll. You were getting the nastiest R&B that existed. They paid for it and made sure it was there, and Hunter was one of the people who represented it. Was it an esteemed thing? You'd better believe it was. That music is an art form, and it's rarely executed. Long John never drank at the Lobby, that I saw. Sometimes on Saturday nights, there would be a small Coke glass with a little something at the bottom, and I could never figure out if it was Coke and rum or what, but as far as I could tell, I don't think he ever drank. When he was in there, he had to do seven and eight hour stretches, night after night. He only took one night off. He was about 6'2", 6'3" and man, could that guy hammer it out unbelievably. Long John Hunter had brought guys with him from East Texas, but the drummer just disappeared, so Miguel the bartender says, 'Why don't you show me how to do that. I can do that.' Within one or two years, he was virtuoso status.

I FOUGHT THE LAW

He was probably the greatest natural-born drummer I've ever seen in my life. Anybody that you talk to who saw him will say that he was one of the most fabulous drummers that ever existed, and it was all because Long John said, "Yeah go ahead, you can play the drums, but I want you to do this, I want you to do that," and he led him along the way, got him started. Miguel was fabulous. Unbelievable. One side of his brain was playing drums and the other side was just cruising down some street in Juarez, Mexico. The guy did this stuff effortlessly. I mean, it's hard to put into words how Long John Hunter stumbled into one of the greatest percussion musical virtuosos of all time that epitomizes the southwest sound. Hunter was the conduit. I'm gonna assume that he never became more than a Mexican national, and disappeared into Mexico. He stayed at the Lobby until themed-1960s. Chicken became a cop in El Paso. They were all so good. They were very accelerated. They played rock and roll with an accelerated Latin beat, in terms of maybe Ritchie Valens on amphetamines. They played the Lobby occasionally, but their main gig was the Chinese Palace. It was one or two blocks down from the Lobby. Very slippery. These places were built in the twenties, and they were built to counteract prohibition in the United States. They were palaces. Some of the woodwork and some of the stuff that was in them was, is still, unbelievable. If you go down there, if you have the guts to go to Juarez, Mexico today, which not many people do. Bad. It's bad. But if you step into one of the bars, you start looking at the beams—these places were palaces. There was a huge old Blanca Beer sign there when John and Little Joe and all those guys played there. I have a picture of Pancho Villa and three of his soldiers in front of the Lobby with the same sign hanging there! So the Lobby had to have been there from the turn of the century. Everything that we know as pop music came from the matrix of rock and roll. What happened in El Paso is very integral in that part. To what degree? Something happened big time there, there's no doubt about it. It affected a lot of the stuff on the west coast, directly. Juarez was blazing in the fifties, early sixties. A lot of the bars and clubs in Juarez were built when liquor was illegal in the United States and people would come down to the borderlands and party for peanuts for a few days, rent a motel room and live it up. The Lobby was a scum bar by the time we were going down there. It was sleazy as hell, but they still put bouncers in there—no cameras, no pictures, nothing. They'd throw people out of there all the time; there were stabbings. I mean it was notorious. Things would go, usually, 'til two or three in the morning, until the bands ran out. Then there is the saga of Little Joe Washington. Was there somebody who was a better guitar player than Hendrix? Yes, there was. He played the the original house Telecaster, the one at the Lobby that Long John Hunter played. They just sanded it off and spray painted it when somebody new would come along. Somebody would say, 'Hey, I want a blue guitar,' and they'd sand it and spray it. I mean we're talking basic elements here. It is just as elusive a story as Robert Johnson. Little Joe was the electric Robert Johnson. The music was at a much higher pace and much high crescendo. Long John left for the west coast to make it big and ended up playing with Etta James. He went out for fame and fortune and gold. He didn't want to blow his brains out in Mexico. He left and they had this kid come through, who appeared on Crosno's Hop, and I remember sitting in front of the TV watching the show. Crosno's beautiful—I mean he put Little Joe on TV and I mean, this guy looked like he'd just fallen off a freight train. He had a sports jacket on that looked like he had slept in it for months. The guy was Little Joe Washington from East Texas. I was like, 'What the hell is this?' Little Joe was on fire. Well, he was… God, I don't want to do injustice to anybody, but he was probably the Black equivalent of Bobby. John was in his early thirties in '65. Little Joe was eight to ten years younger at least. His first time on television, he was a teenager. When he was at the Lobby, which was still in still decline, he was twenty to twenty-one years of age. But something happened during that period. Little Joe Washington had a higher sense of composition than Hendrix. I never saw Hendrix live. I played right next to him but I didn't go in there, 'cause I said, 'Shit. Anybody that's named Jimi that spells their name J-I-M-I, he's probably one of those goddamn hippie guys.' And everybody's going, 'Ciccarelli, God damn it, will you just come out on one of your breaks and walk over to the Whisky?' He was at the Whisky and I was playing at the Galaxy, right next door. This was when Hendrix was just trying to cut loose. Talk about stupidity. I should have listened a little more closely. But at any rate, was Little Joe better than Hendrix? Yeah. Was he years ahead of him? Yes. He fell flat on his face when he came out to California because there was no alcohol, no heroin, no amphetamines, not the support system that you got at the Lobby. I think John was a smart guy. John was, in terms of physical stature, beautiful. He was a beautiful Black man. He was no less than Larry Holmes, Mike Tyson or Muhammad Ali. He was one of these guys who was smart, and he also had physiology. So he never got caught up in drugs, from what I can tell. I never saw him with anything. So he didn't get caught up in it. Some of the other ones did, because the pressure was enormous. John wanted to go to California and he saw greater things, but the lesser ones crumbled in the Lobby. They were like, 'Oh, I can have all of this for nothing?' 'Yeah!' Temptation! The Lobby was the Crossroads. It's not in Mississippi where Robert Johnson sold his soul. It's in Juarez, Mexico in a run down gin mill called the Lobby."

CHAPTER FIVE

THE LOST GOLDMINE

Mother had a bad dream that something terrible had happened to Jack. The police tried to tell her that he was a grown man and was probably somewhere drinking it off.

"It was Sunday February 5, 1961. Mother had finished cooking Sunday dinner. I walked into the kitchen and saw she had a strange look on her face. 'I wonder where Jack is?' she said. 'Oh, don't worry Mother, he'll be here.' She said, 'He's never been late before, he would have called.' I said, 'If he hasn't called, that means he's coming.' Bobby overheard the conversation and said, 'Mother, you worry too much. Jack can take care of himself. He's a big boy now.' Dad arrived home about that time. He had been playing golf, as he did each Sunday. He said, 'What's for dinner?' Bobby said, 'Nothing right now because Mother's upset 'cause our big brother hasn't showed up yet. If we don't eat soon, that fine dinner Mom cooked will be getting cold.' Dad walked away shaking his head, and I overheard him say, 'I've had a strange feeling all day that something bad is gonna happen.' As the evening twilight faded into the dark lonely night, Jack still didn't show.

Mother's worry became infectious to us all. She wouldn't go

to bed, she couldn't stop crying, and every little bit she would say, 'I just know something's awful has happened to Jack.' Trying to make her feel better I would say, 'He's probably just gone over to Juarez and got drunk or something.' She said, 'No! No! No! Oh God no! I just know something awful has happened to Jack.' This went on and on and on, late into the night, until finally she fell asleep for a while. Then Dad, Bobby and I, quietly went to our bedrooms to try to get some much needed sleep.

Just about an hour went by, and Mother woke up suddenly screaming with horror. 'I saw his spirit at the foot of the bed. Jack said he was hit in his head and it killed him!' Mother then went into a state of deep depression. We all would take turns after that telling her it was a bad dream. Go back to sleep and Jack will call tomorrow. Then she would scream again with horror, 'He's dead. He's dead. I know Jack's dead. I saw his spirit at the foot of the bed.'

The next morning, Mother drifted into deeper and deeper depression, and Dad called the family doctor over to give her some medication. Then Dad made some phone calls to find out if Jack might have been in an accident. He contacted the police department. All with no luck. As a last resort, Dad and I went over to Juarez to see if he might be in jail there. Still no luck. Then Dad and I began to worry. When we got home, Dad called the police department again to file a missing persons report. Bobby said Mother finally went to sleep, from a sedative the doctor gave her. So then we all got some rest to face the uncertain future.

As the days passed, there was still no word from Jack. Two detectives came out to the house to talk to Mom and Dad. It was beginning to look like Jack really was missing, and the detectives told Dad, that each day goes by without word, looked more and more like foul play. Bobby and I still had hope know-

I FOUGHT THE LAW

ing Jack the way we did, thought he still could be somewhere in trouble and couldn't call home. Mother though, had lost all hope mainly from the vision she had, of Jack's spirit.

Three weeks later, we got a call from the detectives. They told Dad that the police had arrested a young man driving Jack's '57 Chevy in Lubbock. Although he insisted that he had bought the car from Jack, they suspected foul play. He said he bought the car from Jack, and left him at the border, and didn't know what happened to Jack after that. My Dad then responded, 'That old boy did something to my stepson, because Jack loved and worked too hard in the oil fields for that car to just go and sell it. He just wouldn't do that!'

I don't know why they transferred the young man, twenty-one year old Roy Leon Handy, to Alamogordo, but they did. Then the detectives came by our house again, to ask Dad if maybe he could drive to New Mexico, and talk to Roy Leon Handy and try to get him to confess, or to at least tell us where Jack was.

February 25 was Mother's birthday, and Dad had to go with the detectives to talk to a man that may have killed her first born son. The detectives led Dad into the interrogation room and set Dad down face to face with Roy Leon Handy. Then Dad asked Roy, 'Did you kill my son?' and Roy denied it, and was sticking to his story, about buying Jack's car and letting him off at the border. Dad then said, 'Roy you're lying. Everyone that ever knew Jack, knows he would never sell that '57 Chevy that he worked so hard to buy. You killed him didn't you Roy?' He said, 'No, Mr. Fuller. I'm telling the truth.' Dad said, 'Roy, is your mother living?' He nodded his head and said yes. Dad said, 'How do you think your mother would feel, if someone killed you and left your body in some remote place to decay and the animals to carry off? Please tell us the truth, so we can put Jack to rest properly, so his mother can stop crying and worrying about where he is.'

Roy hung his head and in a low whisper said, 'I killed Jack, Mr. Fuller, and his body is on the Mescalero Indian Reservation, Between Tularosa and Ruidoso, New Mexico.'

Dad broke down and had to be helped out to his car knowing he had to come home and break the tragic news to Mother, Bobby and me.

The story that the detectives got from Roy Handy was that he met Jack early Sunday morning, February 5, at the bus depot. They talked awhile and seemed to have a lot in common so decided to go shooting at targets some in the desert. He said that on the way he saw what looked like thousand dollar bills in Jack's sun visor, and that's what made up his mind to do the evil thing he did. The money in the sun visor wasn't real money at all. It was a present of play money Jack had bought for the little boy who lived next door to him, that reminded him of his own son that he never got to see after he was a year old because of a bitter divorce. Handy also thought he'd get Jack's car out of the deal too. They took turns setting up targets to shoot at. When it was Jack's turn, Handy opened fired on him. He shot him four times while Jack was trying to get away; one in the back of the arm wounding him, three in the back, while he was running, trying to get away from Handy. Then when he could run no more, Handy shot Jack once in the back of the head and killed him, then left his lifeless body there to decay. When they found Jack his pockets were turned inside out. And he was black and bloated so bad you could hardly recognize him.

The local newspapers later reported that Jack and Roy had gone looking for a lost gold mine, as they had found a map in Juarez. The following days were very hard for Bobby, Dad and I. Mother had a complete breakdown and she wasn't getting any better. We were afraid that she might attempt suicide. We all had to take turns watching her. One time in the night, she slipped away, and a man brought her home and said she had tried to jump in front of his car on the highway. Meanwhile, Dad could stand no more of seeing Mom in so much agony and agreed to let her have the shock treatments that doctors were saying she needed. It was pure hell to see here go through that, and even today, I wonder if it actually helped. Finally, over the weeks, she began to improve and the doctor allowed her to come home. She never tried to commit suicide anymore, but she was still suffering from deep depression. Her crying in the night and never sleeping went on a very long time. And I can still hear Mother's words echoing in the back of my brain, 'Oh, God, why, why, did we ever leave Farmington?'"

"Bobby had started as a freshman at North Texas State College in Denton, just up from Dallas," recalls Randy. "When he came home at Easter, he decided he wasn't gonna go back."

Bobby had spent Spring Break, then called Splash Day, on the Gulf Coast in Galveston, where spring holiday festivities had been celebrated by cavorting teenagers since 1911. In May of 1961, pleasantries turned to night time rioting and hundreds of arrests, with 250 cops called in from all around the area. The *Galveston Chronicle* expressed the feelings of one college boy which seemed to reflect the mood of many, 'What a thrill. My mother will disown me. But so what. Now my life is complete—my name's on a police blotter. I don't care if they arrest me again.'

According to Lynn Miley, a Dallas high schooler also partying there, "I met Bob the first of May 1961. I met him in Galveston on Splash Day Weekend. He was a student at North Texas State and I was a senior at Hillcrest High School, and we happened to be staying in the same house that weekend in Galveston. We became very close and actually became engaged. He was my date for Senior Prom and for the Senior All Night party. We used to sit and try to think up names for the band he wanted to form. Some names we came up with were Fuller's Fairies and Bob Fuller and the Empties! He put a down payment on a beautiful diamond ring and then something happened and he went back home to El Paso and I never heard from him again. Needless to say, my heart was broken. I remember he loved his music and his cars. I used to tell him he would never marry me because he was already married to his guitar! I guess I was right!"

"Bobby never mentioned anything to me about being engaged," says Randy. "He told me he didn't like the music program up in Denton and that's why he left. He told Mother and Dad that he wanted to stay around home for school and of course, they were happy about that. Maybe he told Mother about the girl and maybe she talked him out of it. Anyway, he went through the motions and signed up at Texas Western (College in El Paso), but then took the enrollment money and used it to soup up our 1959 Chevy Impala. Bobby didn't like working on cars, but I fixed it up good. Johnny Daniels and I raced against every hot car in town with that Chevy one night, and we beat them all."

El Paso native Rick Stone remembers the Chevy, "It was a '59 Chevy Impala with a 348, with high compression pistons, the works. Man, that car was hopped up—it was hot, beautiful, a silver metallic blue. We timed it that summer on our own drag strip at the old school. There was this natural straightaway that ran the length of our old school building. I mean, it was an ordinary street but we'd stripped out the one way signs and across the pavement in big letters we put BURGES DRAGWAY. At the finish line we painted END over the bus stop sign and we measured off a quarter mile with a bicycle tire. It was great, the drag ended right at the desert and there was nothing there but sand. We'd peel out into the sand and have a blast! One time Bobby borrowed my car, well, my parents' car, and it was this new thing and Bobby had been drinking and had driven out into the desert and puked all over the inside of that car. I had a bit of explaining to do when I got home." The teenage hijinx were about to come to a crashing halt for Randell.

"I'd started dating an ex-girlfriend of Bobby's named Mary Ann," says Randy, "and one thing led to another. She got pregnant. I was seventeen and she was sixteen. I wasn't in love with her and Mother didn't want to sign the court papers to okay the marriage because she knew in her heart it wouldn't last. Dad on the other hand was locked into the old school, and believing heavily in the Ten Commandments, he insisted it was the only decent thing to do. We got married on July 31, 1961, and soon had a daughter we named Kim. We were both still trying to finish high school, but I dropped out. For my own part I just couldn't stand that school, and the pressure of being married and going to school was murder. Dad got me a job at the El Paso Natural Gas Company, so I could support my new family. And he got us a 1960 Corvair for a wedding present. It was my first real set of wheels, after the Allstate motor scooter we bought from Sears. And my bicycle. And me and Bob's '59 Chevy. Me and Mary Ann moved into her grandmother's house down on Lafayette in lower South El Paso. She used to rent out part of her place, a little section off of the main house. You could walk through a door into it from her house, but they always kept it locked.

"Here I was, married, and still in high school. It was the worst. I got kicked out 'cause I cussed the principal out. Yes, I just got sick of him. He made me stand out in the hall for some kind of punishment, and here I am married with a baby, for crying out loud, and I'm out in the hall 'cause I didn't do something right, standing out there like a little kid. I turned around and I saw that principal coming and I flipped him the bird and walked out. "Sorry I had to do that to you," I told him. I never went back. I hated Bel Air High School. I don't blame Bobby for not wanting to go back there. When I stop and think about it, Bel Air was my downfall as far as grades, sports, everything. The coaches, they were jerks. It was a new school and it was in the bad part of town; South El Paso had a lot of punks, Pachuco types—white shirts, khakis. The old gang look and stuff. That's how they dressed and I hated that particular thing. And then the teachers, they just didn't care. The school didn't have any heritage. It was my downfall there, that's all I can say. I went to school in Salt Lake City at these beautiful schools, just beautiful, you wouldn't believe it. We'd sing; they had a singing section, like study hall or something, but you'd go to sing, because they were Mormons. And we'd go to sing songs in there and it was just so wonderful. And it was always an up-spirited kind of thing. You just felt so alive in Salt Lake, I mean at that time, it was just wonderful. And the scenery around it—you were just a hop, skip and a jump away from Jackson Hole, Wyoming, all the wild places. Farmington was just the same way, the schools there, they'd been there for years. I mean, I got eighties when I was in grade school, at those places. I got good grades. In El Paso, I hated school. I hated it. I mean, I never figured anybody could be successful going to school unless they were brainwashed into believing that the only way they were gonna get anywhere is to go to college like the system wants you to. The only thing they taught me in school was the things I don't do today. I really learned all about English on my own, now, as far as writing or spelling. If somebody tells you, 'I before E after C' and all this and then you see other words that contradict that, and you're spelling wrong, and they give you an F. Well wait minute now, not all of them are that way. You can find words that have that interplay, where I is before E or E is before I, and there's no C in the word! You know, I mean it's things like that which drive you nuts. I mean I said hey, I don't need that. I was an outdoor person. I wanted to play football, but I couldn't get the grades. I would've been a heck of a football player for the school team, 'cause I was a heck of a football player around town just on Sundays and things. And everybody would be playing on the field goofing off, and I'd go out and play with the football players and outdo 'em. I'd get a touchdown. Everybody else would be getting tackles. I'd say, 'Gimme that damn ball.' And I'd run all the way for a touchdown. And they're going, 'Man, you ought to play football.' So I go out for football, and what do I do? I sit on the bench 'cause my grades are bad. Bobby's grades weren't so good either, but he always managed to pass. If he got an F, somehow or other he would manage to graduate. Someway or another, he would make it up. Me, I just didn't want to. Period. I hated it all. But then I started thinking, when I got married and I got stuck there in that apartment. I'd be by myself, and Mary Ann would be at work, and I'd be sitting on the bed, thinkin' about what I was gonna do with my life. I didn't have any education to speak of. I had nothing to look forward to other than getting a job like what all these other people were doing. I want to play music with Bobby. I don't want to do this. I was going completely crazy. I mean, really, I was. And I was so depressed about it that the best thing that ever happened was when me and Mary Ann broke up. I would've probably been dead if that didn't happen."

"My dad got me a job at the gas company," continues Randy, "He said, 'You're gonna have to go to work and support your family.' Man, I mean, I said, 'I never done anything like this in my life, and I didn't even want to get married, but you told me I had to.' My mother wouldn't have made me. I felt like I just didn't have any future. I was really messed up. It was really killing me. But I went to work in the mailroom at Dad's company as a mail router and they had a machine with cards, an IBM thing. I had no confidence and felt stuck, with no future and meanwhile, all these things were happening for Bobby. People would say, 'Bobby Fuller? He's your brother? Man, he's something else.' Well, you know, it wasn't really a younger brother thing, 'cause we were so close. It was more like, 'He has everything going and you're just a big nothing.' It was more like that. I don't know what it was. It wasn't always like that. It really started in El Paso. Well, it maybe it kinda started in Salt Lake City, but you know, I still had all my friends there and I was going to a great school. In El Paso, there was nothing for me, period. I mean, it was... you'd get days when the wind would blow, and sand would be blowing across the street, and the clouds were a certain way, and it just seemed like there was never anything good ever gonna happen. It was a hopeless place. It was hopeless from the day we got there.

"And I would be in the house, there, with Mary Ann and the baby, and I'd say, 'I gotta get out of here.' And all I would do is get in my car, and I'd drive all the way to northeast El Paso, watching the sand blow across the desert by the airport, and watch rabbits and wild things run across the road, and then I'd drive all the way over there where the teen club was and turn around and drive home. That was my thrill. Other than goin' hunting. For me, I'd mostly go hunting by myself with a gun. I'd shoot snakes, rabbits, ground squirrels. To this day, I wish I had never killed any of them. I would never do that again. When you're kids, back then, that's what you did. The boys, the whole town, all the kids hunted. They had a .22 or a shotgun, and they'd go out in the desert and hunt rabbits, or deer, if they were in season. There just wasn't nothing else to do there, I mean except for music for us, and that just became the most wonderful thing, you know. I would come in from nothing happening. I'd come home to the Album Avenue house and Bobby would be in there, and he'd say, 'Hey, c'mon, put some bass on this.' Well, I mean, it was great, 'cause it would be just me and him there playing music.

One night, I got a call from an old friend of my brother's, Johnny Daniels. He wanted to know if I wanted to play bass at a gig with him and two other old friends of mine, Johnny Elston and Phil Engling. I accepted. Johnny Daniels was kind of like the Fonzie of our day, a Hells Angel wannabe. The gig was a dance at the Radford school for girls, and their boyfriends were invited. We played a set and went all right. Johnny Daniels sounded a lot like Ritchie Valens. On the break, Johnny Daniels whispered in my ear, 'Hey Randell, let's go outside. I want you to see something.'

"Johnny led me around to the side of the school, under a tree. There was a dim light shining from an empty classroom. He opened his hand and said, 'Randell, have you ever tried one of these?' When I looked into his hand, I saw what looked like three small toothpicks. I said, 'What! Toothpicks, of course.' He said, 'No man, grass, Mary Jane.' Finally I got the picture. I said, 'No, and don't want to.' I knew then that's probably why Bobby quit playing with him. My folks had raised us to be totally against drugs. About that time Johnny Elston and Phil Engling came around the corner and with low whispering voices, said, 'Y'all getting high?' and started laughing. They had already torched one up and got high before the gig started. I said, 'Not me, but Daniels is.' They immediately joined in smoking with

Johnny Daniels. This took me completely off guard. Not on Johnny's behalf, because there was always talk around town that he smoked pot, but I was surprised that Johnny and Phil did. As they puffed away, they kept insisting that it didn't hurt you. It wasn't like the dreaded heroin that addicted you and then made you so deathly sick. So I gave it a try. After a few hits off the joint, I started laughing so hard I thought I'd never stop. And with all the crap that had been going on in my life that felt good. When we went back to finish playing the gig though, I couldn't figure out one key from another. I couldn't stop laughing, so I just sat down on my amplifier and pretended to know what the hell I was doing. But I didn't.

"Back home, I had put some pot in the dresser drawer in our bedroom, and Mary Ann's mother came in and went through my clothes and stuff. Her mother had Mary Ann call me up in Fresno, Texas in Fort Bend County. She said, 'They're gonna take the baby away from you. You've had it, they're gonna call the sheriff and you're goin' to jail.' You know, I'm sayin', 'You tell your mother and everybody to stay outta my stuff. It's none of their damn business.' And then we moved out of the grandmother's house when I got back, to a place in the lower valley, to little house with wood paneling. It looked like a little cabin. It was all right for a while, but Mary Ann was just too intense. She made me go with her where she wanted to go, and didn't let me do anything without her. We moved again over on Trowbridge. Boyd Elder lived just a few blocks away.

CHAPTER SIX

ONLY FOR YOU
There was something about the desert and the wind and
the radio, the way it wrapped itself around your brain.
It was a lonely feeling, kinda like not remembering who you are.

By 1962, Bobby had already seen action on the regional Yucca label as the uncredited drummer for the Embers (with future BF4 members Jim Reese and Dalton Powell), having recorded both sides *Almost Blue* and *Jim's Jive* in his bedroom on an Ampex rig brought in by KHEY radio engineer Rod Matthews. Subsequently, that group ended up backing Bobby on a pair of custom press original composition solo sides recorded in the Fuller living room—the utterly Hollyesque *Guess We'll Fall In Love* backed with the upbeat *You're In Love*, co-crafted by Bobby with neighbor lady Mary Stone. Local clatter shot this first solo effort to #2 local radio station KELP by Easter, with legendary DJ Steve Crosno at the wheel, bolstering Bobby into trading the drum throne to front his own combo on guitar. By this time, Randy was home from school and was promptly drafted in on bass. This came both as a surprise and disappointment to the younger Fuller, who assumed he'd have a shot at the guitar slot, now taken by Bobby. Randy was to develop into one of truly great bass players in rock and roll,

I FOUGHT THE LAW

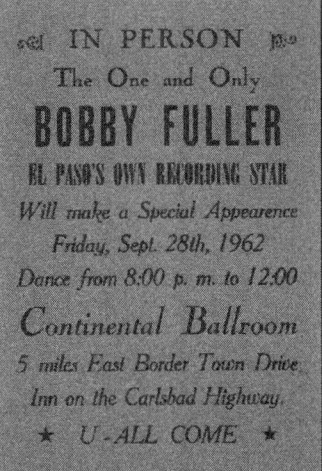

LEFT: *Bobby, Mr. Rock and Roll*

and it is his inventive, percussive lines that would serve to propel the group into the national charts.

Bobby's first published interview was in the Rancer Roundup, the mimeographed Ross Intermediate School newspaper, on March 30, 1962. In it he said he had one record out, *You're In Love*, and that a new record was due out in two weeks. He also stated for the record that his dream was to visit Easter Island, that his favorite movie was Spartacus, and that he would like to have Jerry Lewis's humor and Judy Garland's performing ability, and that his favorite pastimes were waterskiing and chess. He claims in this interview to have met Zsa Zsa Gabor, although that claim has not been corroborated.

Randy would make his first record appearance accompanying Bobby on twin teeners, cut under the aegis of Buddy Holly's mentor Norman Petty, with Mrs. Vi Petty on keys and a studio tapper on traps, at his studio in Clovis, New Mexico. It was Bobby's adoration of Buddy Holly that was behind this move. "Bobby's big thing," said Jim Reese, "was Buddy Holly.

I FOUGHT THE LAW

Don't get me wrong, I thought the world of Bobby Fuller and I cared a lot for him, so I say this with the best intentions—but he was into Buddy Holly so much that if Buddy Holly decided to wear one red sock and one blue sock and Bobby Fuller found out about it, Bobby Fuller would've had one red sock and one blue sock. He figured that the only way to accomplish whatever Buddy Holly had accomplished was to be as much like Buddy Holly as possible."

"Bobby booked the session and he and I and Jim Reese drove five hours across New Mexico to record a song that Bobby had written called *Gently My Love* and another one called *My Heart Jumped*," recalls Randy. "Norman Petty's wife Vi played piano, Bobby and Jim played guitar, and I played bass. Jimmy Gilmer was in the studio at the time recording his new album and hit single, *Sugar Shack*. I think Norman Petty took

LEFT: *Bobby, teen idol*

I FOUGHT THE LAW

RIGHT:
Ready to rock

Jimmy Gilmer in under his wing to try to make another star like Buddy Holly."

The flip of *Gently, My Love* was *My Heart Jumped* by Dick Liberatore, a music lover who went on to marry Alan Freed's daughter. "From March 1961 through July 1962 I was based at Holloman Air Force Base in Alamogordo, New Mexico," says Dick, "about 90 miles out of El Paso. I was in charge of providing entertainment for the servicemen on the base that included a monthly dance. Bobby called and expressed interest in performing for one of our monthly dances. I asked him to send me info about himself, which he did. Sight unseen, I booked him in January 1962. After setting up that afternoon I asked if he would be interested in hearing a song that I wrote. He said yes, and I played and sang *My Heart Jumped* which he immediately liked and expressed interest in recording. I later discovered that he did record the song at the Norman Petty Stu-

I FOUGHT THE LAW

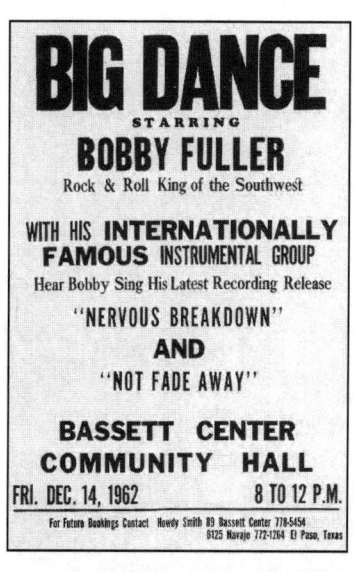

BIG DANCE
STARRING
BOBBY FULLER
Rock & Roll King of the Southwest

WITH HIS **INTERNATIONALLY FAMOUS** INSTRUMENTAL GROUP
Hear Bobby Sing His Latest Recording Release

"NERVOUS BREAKDOWN"
AND
"NOT FADE AWAY"

BASSETT CENTER COMMUNITY HALL
FRI. DEC. 14, 1962   8 TO 12 P.M.
For Future Bookings Contact Howdy Smith 89 Bassett Center 778-5454
6125 Navajo 772-1264 El Paso, Texas

dios in Clovis, New Mexico and the song was released on Yucca Records in June 1962. That was the same time I was transferred to Elmendorf Air Force Base in Alaska, so I had no idea that the song had been recorded and released until I came across a Bobby Fuller album ten years ago and happened to see that my song listed on it, for which I had not received one thin dime. During my fifteen months in New Mexico, Yucca released another one of my songs titled *Why Did You Leave Me* which I also produced. And we also recorded two other songs that I wrote, *Only For You* and *Platonic Girl*. Both were not released but somehow Bobby got hold of *Only For You* which he later went on to record."

At any rate, working at the Petty studio with Vi Petty tinkling away at the piano could have been at least inspirational for Bobby. Still, despite the hallowed location and the Holly vibes, the resultant sides are tepid at best.
Songwriter Eddie Reeves recalls with chagrin his early experience recording *When Sin Stops* with Norman Petty in 1958, where Petty spend hours recording numerous takes of their songs, pressing the energy out of them, "Years later, I realized Petty's process was counter to the very essence of rock and roll, which is at minimum a spontaneous emotional explosion of teenage feelings and thoughts and one not planned and carefully hammered out by adult engineering seeking form and coherence."

Early-on Fuller fan James Leslie echoes the thoughts of

I FOUGHT THE LAW

Eddie Reeves regarding Norman Petty's attitude toward young musicians and music fans, "I was born in Clovis, New Mexico but moved as a kid to Carlsbad. We would visit Clovis on holidays and during the summer because my grandparents were still there, as well as the rest of our family. My granddad owned the Clovis Monument Company next door to Nor-Va-Jack Studios on 7th Street. One day in 1960, when I was ten, I was at Woolworth looking at the records and saw the Buddy Holly Story LP, and on the back it said he recorded in Clovis and that Norman Petty had produced him. I knew my grandmother lived across the alley from his mother, Mrs. Petty, and that she was good friends with Grandma. I asked if I could meet him and they said I could, the next time he come over. That happened soon afterward, and he brought me into the living room and showed me all of his sheet music for his songs and the Norman Petty album with *Almost Paradise* on it. He told me if I wanted a career as a musician I should go to college and major in music and learn to read music so that I could get a job as a music teacher. I think my parents might have asked him to say that because that's what they believed. He never mentioned Buddy Holly or any other rock and roll acts he produced. That really puzzled me cause I knew he worked with Buddy Holly. I was so mad he didn't say anything about it, that it made me determined to be musician and not read music. My other grandmother also lived in Clovis and she was good friends with George Tomsco of the Fireballs' mother. She invited us over for dinner when I was about 13 and I spoke to George all evening about becoming a picker. He was a lot more positive about it but told me I would have to have a day job even though he didn't at the time. I still hold a grudge for Norman being so self centered and only talking about himself."

Although there was nary a semblance of neither *Thunder* or roar in the Petty productions, Randy feels that it was a great experience, "We learned how Norman's echo chambers were so valuable to the sound he was getting. We also saw he was using Neumann u67 microphones. When we got home, we poured a forty by four foot slab of cement in the back yard up against a rock wall and built a two by four frame four foot high and four foot wide with plywood siding with shingles on top for roofing. On the inside we nailed linoleum on the sides and on the ceiling, then stuck a mike at one end, and a speaker at the other, hoping to get a unique sound. It worked out well, especially when mixed with tape echo and Fender reverb chambers. But since the sound traveled through the chamber fairly loudly, the neighbors complained sometimes late at night. After we finished, we cut a rectangular shaped window between the den and control booth, and installed glass so as to be able to communicate with one another. Later on we found out you get a lot more delay if you don't make the walls parallel. Bobby couldn't stop thinking about those Neumann mikes that Norman Petty used, so he talked Mother into getting Dad to co-sign to buy a couple of them. Today, if you can find one, they are valued in the thousands of dollars. I think we paid two hundred each for the ones we bought That was a lot of money at the time, but what a difference in the vocals! And they sounded great on other instruments like piano, drums and acoustic guitar—well worth the money. We recorded all that summer and started to get along for a change after being apart for a year."

The Fuller home studio consisted of a tiny control booth constructed into the back of their attached garage, and a window mounted into the wall to face the makeshift den studio. An echo chamber was crafted out of a slab of concrete and a roll of linoleum set up, lean-to style, the full length of the side of the house. This primitive set-up managed to deliver fabulous, raucous recordings thanks to the newly financed Ampex four-track tape recorders and a late date trick bag of devices that Bobby could employ thanks to his day job at the Melody Shop at the nearby Bassett Center. When the Fender Reverb GA-15 arrived on the market, Bobby got his hands on it at the Melody Shop and never let go. Likewise when the first Maestro FZ-1 fuzztone units shipped, Bobby grabbed one by the horns and put it on his work tab.

"We had wires all over the house," recalled Loraine Fuller in 1988. Behind a large painting on the den wall was the glass panel of Bobby's control booth. The den area itself was about eighteen feet square, with a sliding glass door that opened to a patio; another wall featured a brick fireplace with shelves alongside it that still held some of Bobby's record collection, made up Elvis, Eddie Cochran, Everly Brothers, Buddy Holly and Gene Vincent records.

Even though there was music going on all the time in the Fuller home, the neighbors were all reasonably tolerant. "I can recall one time when people complained," said Mrs. Fuller, "The police came over, but they ended up liking the music, and they even stayed a while to listen." Bobby was always concerned with the quality of the sound he was coming up with.

I FOUGHT THE LAW

Rick Stone recalls, "I went over to the Fullers when they had just gotten home with these theatre speakers. I was totally overpowered by the sound. At that time, even the theatres in El Paso didn't have speakers like that!" Meanwhile, Bobby was also lugging his tape recorder along when he went to check out other bands. "Bobby had been taking his tape recorder to shows for years," said Jim Reese, "He studied those tapes and he listened to records he liked the sound of, like Buddy Holly records, and he tried to duplicate the sound himself at home."

Bobby, 1961

Meanwhile, creating the perfect band presented problems for Bobby, who wanted only the best, most dedicated guys in the combo that he had dubbed the Fanatics. Band slots got filled by a revolving cast of able friends early on, beginning with drummer Gaylord Grimes, who served dutifully in the summer of '62 just as Jim Reese opted in from the Embers for a ten day Big Dipper Lounge lead guitar stint. The lounge had lost its liquor license for ten days and Bobby had persuaded the owner into turning the Dipper into a teen club for the duration of the suspension.

"It's funny how all these things happen," said Jim. "Just that day I had seen a car I really wanted, so when Bobby asked me, I asked him what my share of the money would be and he said a hundred bucks and that's exactly what I needed as a down payment on the car, so I said okay."

I FOUGHT THE LAW

It should be noted that Jim had been playing non-stop during the months he wasn't playing with the Fuller brothers. He had played guitar on Jerry Bright's 45 *Rosie/Indian Giver* on Jerry's own Bright label, and also on the Counts instrumental *Chug A Lug / Surfer's Paradise*, which had Bobby Taylor on drums, Sonny Fletcher on rhythm guitar and Howard Steel on bass. About the B-side, Jim says, "We didn't know what to name it, so we added some surf sounds and bird sounds and named it *Surfer's Paradise*. What the hell, if you can't lick 'em, join 'em!" About the Jerry Bright 45, he adds, "Jerry hired me, Dalton and Randy Widener to go to Petty Studio in Clovis to do a couple of Chuck Berry numbers but Petty talked Jerry into doing these. Rosie has a real cool sound to it, but the background vocals bug me, and Indian River is best described as, well—it sucks!"

The ten day stint at the bowling alley was a huge success, the band's lineup being Bobby, Randy and Jim and at first trusty but college-bound Gaylord Grimes, who Bobby traded in for Morris "Googie" Dirmeyer, who was replaced by Dalton Powell when poor Googie, who was working for a local elevator firm, got a finger lopped off in an Otis incident. Dalton, although then banging the piano for the Embers, had been itching for a chance to pound the skins.

On July 21, 1962 the *Xmas In July* dance in Hueco was billed as "Bobby Fuller and his Combo." Admission was $2 plus 50 cents per guest for chips, beer and booze, with "Bourbon and Scotch furnished." By September, he had become, "The One and Only Bobby Fuller, El Paso's Own Recording Star" at a show at the Continental Ballroom on Carlsbad Highway. "U-ALL COME" said the handbill.

So here it was, 1962, and the final BF4 lineup was thrilling kids with rock and roll. Throughout the rest of the year, the band honed their act locally at the Dipper, as well as at the Golden Key Club, Teen A Go-Go, and Bolero Lanes. They were also featured on KELP DJ Steve Crosno's TV show CROS- NO'S HOP, which did a lot to hip teens to Bobby and the band. And that's just what he did, coupling Buddy Holly with Eddie and coming up with his best effort yet. *Not Fade Away/Nervous Breakdown* was issued on his own Eastwood label, named after the section of El Paso he lived in. Bobby milked his in-house wireworks for every volt the patchwork system could muster. It is Jim Reese who plays the guitar leads on the Cochran/Holly double tribute threat, an offering of magnificent performance and superb sound, packaged with a worship-worthy silver-embossed maroon label and promoted straight out of the gate with a big Eastwood High School show and dance, as well as at area holiday blasts which included a holly hop at the Bassett Center Community Hall. The Eastwood label would also host releases recorded by Bobby in his garage by local combos the Chancellors and the Sherwoods.

Jim Gallomore, an original fan going back to Bobby's earliest days on the traps, professed, "Bobby was probably one of the most talented people that I have ever known. I remember the time at Irvin High when he played drums for the Embers and did a ten minute solo. Yow, that was amazing. When he started playing guitar and fronting the band, his abilities became more apparent. He had the best people working with him which made him and them the biggest draw in the region. Buddy would have been proud of the tribute and respect Fuller displayed playing those great tunes like *Peggy Sue*, *Maybe Baby* and *That'll Be The Day*. The first time I remember talking to Bobby was in early '62 at a club in Juarez at The Lobby. I was there celebrating my 16th birthday with some of my friends when Bobby showed up with his running mates. I was introduced to him by a mutual friend, Phil Engling. Although I was just a kid and Bobby was a major talent, he still was pleasant and not at all into the egocentric behavior that sometimes people display. He sat in with Long John's band while Long John Hunter sat with us and talked about how Bobby was going to make the big time! Hunter was so right about that. It was a great time to be involved in the El Paso music scene, and let me say how lucky I feel to have been there. I left EP in May of '63 to go into the USAF. I missed the part where the Fullers found nation-wide fame but I was glad to have been there in the early days. I was based in Germany we used to listen to a radio program that played the *Billboard* Top 10 rock and roll tunes. Imagine my surprise when in February of 1966 they played *I Fought The Law*. Fantastic. What a moment!"

By the end of 1962, life for Randy, who was juggling work, a new family, and playing clubs at night with Bobby and the band, was coming to a head.

"My job at the gas company fell through, because the department I worked in was moving to Odessa," recalls Randy. "For a moment, I thought Bobby and I could make a living playing in clubs. Well, Dad had other plans for me. He said, 'Boy, you can't play music now, you got to support your family. You can't do that playing music.' I down right got so mad, I had to leave the room. But I knew that Dad was always right. It was hopeless. I had to toe the line. He said he would get me a job in Hobbs, New Mexico, on an oil rig. So with a broken spirit, and with my dreams dead in the water, Dad and I left for Hobbs. On the way, a storm moved in and it started snowing something terrible, and it kept up all the way to Hobbs. We checked into a motel where a lot of roughnecks stayed. We went up to our room and Dad started to clue me in on what I was suppose to do. I had never worked on a drilling rig before, and I kept thinking about things my mother had always said. She'd said, 'I hope you and Robert never have to work on those old greasy and dangerous drilling rigs like your dad and Jack did. It's a wonder they hadn't lost a hand or finger like some of their fellow workers, or burned to death in a gas well fire.' Well on top of two feet of snow on the ground and me being hot-tempered and scared, and Dad telling how they were going to tease me because I was a greenhorn, I just had to back out. That's the second time my Dad almost cried. But this time I had to do what I felt was right, in my heart. So with Dad standing there with tears in his eyes, I got into that white Corvair, and in the snowstorm, drove back to my passion—to play rock and roll with my brother for the rest of my life.

Not long after coming back from Hobbs, Mary Ann and I split up for good. We were too young, and we weren't in love. I moved back into the house on Album so that Bobby and I could concentrate strictly on our music.

CHAPTER SEVEN

WINTER SURFIN'
Shopping centers, bowling alleys, high school
hops, dreaming of big blue oceans where
there's nothing but big white sands.

There was a lull in home recording in the early months of 1963, as Bobby had managed to land an extended tour of the Southwest on the strength of regional chart action with *Not Fade Away* and *Nervous Breakdown*. Bobby, Randy, Jim and Dalton ventured as far west as Fresno, California where the band had a stint for several weeks at a country and western club. They returned home to El Paso only briefly, and then left again for a three week club gig in Hobbs, New Mexico.

Says Jim Reese, "I remember one night at the club in Hobbs, Mr. and Mrs. Fuller had come out for the show and they were in the audience and when we were out on stage somebody yelled out at me 'YOUR FLY'S DOWN!' and I was embarrassed out of my mind but Mr. Fuller sort of saved the day for me. See, he has this real deep, gravelly, froggy voice and he yells out 'It's okay, ladies, he's just advertising!' Back in El Paso, Bobby began experimenting even more with his studio. Jim and Dalton were playing in a number of other groups, including a stint backing a black guy known only as 'Jackson.' "We played all these wild black nightclubs," recalls Jim. "This is about when I really started appreciating black audiences! They were totally into the music and out to have a good time."

By this time, there were bands everywhere and local shopping centers were featuring frequent Battles of the Bands. Showing up for the prize money were combos like Ray and the Valiants, Joe Ritchie and the Rooks, and the Intruders, but Bobby was already billing himself as "The Rock and Roll King of the Southwest" and winning the battles with ease. He was also recording many of the local bands, and even issued records for a couple of them on his own label. Rod Crosby of the Intruders recalls Bobby inviting his band in for a free session at the home studio, a move that is believed to have been an effort on Bobby's part to see how the band sounded in the studio, as he was always watching and listening to his competition to see what he could learn.

Future Led Zeppelin sound engineer Terry Manning had befriended Bobby at a local concert, and the two had started exchanging ideas about songs and recording, the elder and more experienced Fuller providing insight to the naive younger devotee. He recalls his friendship with Bobby, and how he brought the El Paso sound to Memphis as a teenager: "If you heard a record on the local radio, that was your world, so Joe Richie's *Across The Bay*, and any record that was played on KELP, was a monster hit to me. My first band was Terry Manning and the Wild Ones. I don't know, but I guess I was the one coaxing some kind of vocal out so it was my name on top of the Wild Ones. I went to Austin High School in El Paso and before that, Bassett Middle School, where I had a crush on the girl who sat in front of me who was kinda cute. I would kind of poke at her and mess with her, and finally she'd had enough, and she turned around and took her pencil and stabbed me in the knee. The lead is still visible there today. So one day the teacher says that we're having a school dance, and that everyone has to attend and bring somebody, and that a parent has to chaperone us. This was to get us started in love or whatever. So I asked the girl in front of me because we all had to go, and she said okay. So we went to this school dance and Bobby Fuller is playing. I knew the girl as Stephanie Nicks. She became Stevie Nicks many years later. So Stevie, or Stephanie, and I are in there. I didn't then, and haven't now, danced. I mean, I don't dance! So we sort of stood around for a bit and finally I said, 'I'm gonna go up and talk to the band. Do you mind?' She shrugged and sat around in the corner the whole time, just sittin' there, and I went up with the band and sat in and played with Bobby and sang *Peggy Sue*. Poor Stephanie. After that, I started talking to Bobby a lot. He was few years older at the time, but it seemed huge. One year younger or older; when you're that age it seems big. Bobby didn't have a band name at that time. He was just Bobby Fuller. When I went to Austin High the next year, he played a dance in our cafeteria. I remember looking at his equipment, thinking, 'Oh, an Alamo amp! I got to get me one of those.' So years later I got me an Alamo amp. So anyway, I started talking to Bobby a lot after that, going to his place, and I guess I wasn't completely a stupid kid then or something, 'cause he embraced me in some way. That studio they built, it was really in the living room, and they had kind of built a little echo thing out in back. It was fantastic, for the day, it was amazing. You know, we became good friends and would talk long hours—long, long hours about songs and different things. I never was *in* his band, but I'd sit in occasionally. And then I wanted to start my own band. He was my big hero because he did everything—he had his own record label, he had his own club, he was just like wow, he's the idol to aspire to be. The last time I saw him was at Skylanes Bowling Alley on Dyer Street. And he was sitting there, he had just been to Nashville, trying to get something going and it just hadn't worked for him. And he came back and he was *so* depressed and *so* down. My dad was a minister and they would move us every two or three years, and one of the places they offered Dad to move was Memphis. I had bought a 45 of *Last Night* by the Mar-Keys on the Satellite label, so when he suggested Memphis, I thought, *there's a record company there!* I was instantly lobbying *Memphis, Memphis, Memphis!* The other option was Fairhope, Alabama, and I had never heard of a record company there! When I saw Bobby at this bowling alley, my family had just decided that we were going to Memphis. Bobby was saying, 'Well I'm gonna try LA. Nashville didn't work, this is my last chance.' He was so down. And I said, 'I'm going to Memphis because there are records there.' He said, 'Well, good luck.' And then within a week, we both had left town. But he was *so* down. I always wondered, *what if?*"

"KELP radio's—and TV's—Steve Crosno was quite a character," continues Terry, "he was the #1 guy who made local records happen in the Southwest. I would listen to him on the radio at night, and I'd call up the station and talk to him. I was the ultimate fan-kid. Finally he said, 'Well, come on by the station. I'll let you do some stuff.' He did live remotes downtown at a clothing store or a bowling alley, advertising, '*Come on down to the so-and-so store today and meet Steve Crosno!*' My first little job with him was to hook up the wires and talk to the station on the telephone. One day, he said, 'You're doing pretty good. Come on by the TV station and we'll let you start doing some stuff there.' The very first day I came in, he said, 'We got somebody comin' in and you're gonna get to go to work. You're gonna help set up the microphone and do all this stuff.' I said, 'Oh great!' Well, it was the great Gene Pitney-- the very first music thing I officially worked on was Gene Pitney! I said to myself, 'This is the greatest!' Gene was out there in front of the cameras miming, but he made it look like it was real. I couldn't believe my eyes. People say rock and roll was at a low point in the US in 1963-64, but in El Paso, it was at its peak. So anyway, we moved toMemphis. I *immediately* got on the bus and went to Stax—Satellite Stax, you know, and just got in the door. If you listen to the middle of *Not Fade Away*, you will hear a telephone ring. That's me calling. I didn't know he was recording at that time, of course, and Bobby said they forgot to take the phone off like they always did. Every time they'd hit 'record', they'd take the phone off, 'cause it would ring, so when I called, somebody just grabbed it and threw it so it only rang one time. And I heard, *I'm gonna tell you how it's gonna be*—I guess that ring was my first appearance on a record! And you know when he had a record on Yucca- wow! That was as big as you can get, I thought. There was a good record selection at the Harmony Shop at the Bassett Center in El Paso. That's where I would go, there or a federal store at the army base—my dad was a minister so we could buy things at a discount there. It was like an early Walmart type thing, and they had a big selection. They had musical instruments, in addition to records, and guitars would be hanging just barely out of reach. One of the guitars that Bobby had was hanging there and I would always eye it and beg and of course my dad wouldn't go for it. Those guitars all had what we now know as the whammy bar, the tremolo bar. Once I pointed up at one and asked the sales guy, 'what's that?' and he said 'that's a Stratocaster.' So for years, even after I'd gotten to Memphis, I thought the *bar* was called a Stratocaster. I'd started playing on a cheap Airline from Montgomery

I FOUGHT THE LAW

Ward's. I just started banging it out on that, learning chords, doing stuff, and I just progressed on my own. I was a Buddy Holly fanatic first and foremost. Everybody was—Texas was *Buddy World*. Buddy Holly was *everything*. I never saw him in person or anything, but we just lived and ate and breathed Buddy, that was the whole thing. I was so young and just getting into it, and it was really the local scene that prompted everything. Now when the Beach Boys came out with their first local record *Surfin'*, and then of course the first album on Capitol and everything—they were big locally in El Paso, too. Some people thought they were too pansy, not rock enough, but a lot of us really were into what they were doing. And Bobby was too. So uh, those were the big influences of the day.

A couple years after we moved to Memphis, I was in the Gentrys studio for two days. What happened was their keyboard player quit and they had a tour booked with *Keep On Dancing*. You know, later I heard that Bobby Fuller's *Let Her Dance*, which came out the right after the Gentrys record did, was originally called *Keep On Dancing* and I wondered if he had changed the title because the Gentrys record became such a huge hit. Anyway, right when the Gentrys were happening locally, I was playing keyboards in Lawson and Four More and I get a call from Larry Raspberry of the Gentrys saying, 'We need a keyboard player, can you come do the tour?' I thought, 'I've made it!' So I go to a practice with them and we're doin' stuff and I go home and tell my mom, 'I'm going on tour.' And she says, 'oh no, you're not. You are not going anywhere.' 'But mom!' I'm crying and everything. 'I can't quit the band.' Well, no more tears, I decided. I was kinda young, but I soon moved out and got my own place.

Then, I got together with Alex Chilton, who was about to become the new lead singer for Ronnie and the Devilles, which was one of the big local Memphis bands. I had just been in town a short while from El Paso and went with the Devilles to American Recording Studio, Chip Moman's place, where the Box Tops ended up recording all their stuff. The Devilles were the guys who morphed into the Box Tops. So Ronnie Jordan, who I worked with, was a good friend, a local DJ and lead singer for Ronnie and the Devilles. Well, Ronnie didn't like something that was going on in the studio, and was disgusted, and was gonna quit the band, so Alex was coming to audition as their new lead singer. Well, but he was late because didn't know where to go or something, so they're going, 'We gotta do something, let's start playing.' So I said, 'You guys know *I Fought The Law*?' So I got on the mike as the lead singer of the Devilles and we start doing *I Fought The Law*, you know, bringing El Paso to Memphis. Well Chips Moman, at this time, is in the top ten on *Billboard*, rivaling all of the hits, this great producer of everything from Elvis to Neil Diamond to Dusty Springfield to whatever, he comes in and he's going, 'This record's a hit! It's great! Let's cut it! You're the singer, forget that other guy.' And we're just standing there, kinda shocked, 'Uh, well Mr. Moman, it's already a hit. Bobby Fuller from where I came from in El Paso has this in the top ten.' Then Alex walked in, end of that story."

The time had come for Bobby to test the waters on the West Coast. Surf music was ruling the planet in '63. *Pipeline, Bust Out, Wipeout* and a slew of other surf instrumentals were riding the charts and it was now or never time. Randy tells the story, "Bobby and I decided to go to California to play some shows and try to meet with a record company, if fate allowed. Dalton couldn't make the trip, and neither could Jimmy Wagnon, so we took a drummer named Freddy Paz along, plus our other guitar player, Tex Reed, 'cause Jim couldn't go. We bought a 1955 Ford station wagon and rented a U-haul, loaded up our music equipment and left El Paso for good old Hollywood. Right after we arrived there, we met these two brothers who were booking agents. They took a chance and booked us on the beach at the old Hermosa Biltmore Hotel in Hermosa Beach. They wanted us to play surfing music for all the surfers that came in at night to dance. We got free rooms there, plus free meals and beer, and we got to lay around on the beach all day and surf and learn the surfers' ways. It gave us a chance to stay longer than we could have otherwise. We didn't have to play on Monday and Tuesday, so those days we would drive into Hollywood and hit all the record companies. We left our copies of our records at Capitol, RCA and several other top labels. Bobby really felt we had a shot. Freddy would later recall that Bobby used to always talk about how ' if Ricky Nelson can make it, so can I'. We ran out of records and then the guys who were booking our shows said we should play something for the record companies that wasn't already a record."

Bobby immediately wrote to his dad. A postcard home from Hermosa Beach dated July 7, 1963, reads: "High there! Please send those tapes to me right away. We are going to take them to Liberty Records... Love, Bob."

"They wouldn't let us get past the receptionist at Liberty," recalls Randy, "They said to leave to leave them and they would make sure the right person got them. After almost a month of waiting, it seemed obvious that they were never going to call. We went and got the tapes back and took them to a guy we had met named Richard Delvy. He was the drummer in a surf group called the Challengers and was really big into that kind of music."

"Bobby brought me some terrific material that he'd recorded back in Texas," said Richard. "I was very interested in working with him, but the next thing I knew, he'd signed with Bob Keene at Del-Fi. I was really surprised and a bit disappointed."

"We had gone to every label we could find in the phone book—twice—but finally Bobby said, 'Come on! Let's go back to Hollywood and talk to Bob Keene at Del-Fi records again," says Randy. "Then, let's drive out to Redondo Beach and check out the Rendezvous and get some ideas of how teen clubs operate."

"We walked into Del-Fi's front office on Selma Street and introduced ourselves to Millie Hemphill, Bob Keene's secretary. As we were asking for an appointment to play Bob our stuff, he came out of his office and Millie introduced him to us. To our amazement Bob asked us to come into his office where he had a two track Ampex so he could hear what we had going. He listened to everything on our demo tape and said, 'Boys, I think you got something good going here but you're not quite ready yet. Go back home and practice for a year and come back out and see me.' Then we left, feeling totally rejected, and drove out to the Rendezvous Ballroom. Dick Dale wasn't there at the time, so we just looked around, and I suppose Bobby was visualizing what was soon to come in El Paso—his own teen center. The we drove back to the Hermosa Biltmore Hotel, and as we were getting out of the car, these surfers came up and started talking to us, giving us compliments on our playing which after all the negative crap in Hollywood that went down, improved our confidence somewhat. Then they talked about a band down on another beach that they liked also, a new band called the Beach Boys. If we knew that they were going to have the success that they did, we probably would have taken the time to go see them. Well, our time out west was finished and besides I got in a fight with the two brothers who were our managers, because I took all the beer from the kitchen's icebox for the band. The younger of the two brothers came into my room and started yelling at me. I was laying on my bed and threw a beer bottle at him. It stuck in the wall next to his head and he ran out and got his big brother. He came in and started yelling, so I kicked his ass Texas style. The next day we went back to El Paso."

Bob Keene says he remembered the visit by the Fuller brothers, " I told them to go home and come back, because I heard the stuff and I said, 'There's something there, but I don't hear a hit record.' That was all I was interested in. I know they'd been to RCA and a couple other labels, which turned him down. I think he got turned down by Liberty, too. So I knew I wasn't the first one he came to."

The turn-down at Liberty, home of Bobby Vee, Eddie Cochran, Jan and Dean, and Del Shannon, among others, would switch around a year or so later, when label boss Al Bennett, who had originally nixed the then-unknown Ventures, only to finally sign them, less than two years later. Had Bob Reisdorff or Snuff Garrett been in the Liberty offices at 6920 Sunset the day the Fullers had come by shopping their music, Bobby and Randy might have sparked their interest. Ironically, it was Snuff Garrett who would issue a Sonny Curtis solo album featuring his composition *I Fought The Law*—right after Bobby's passing in 1966.

Bobby returned home to Texas with a burning desire to help the weary ones to see the light by recreating the wild California surf scene right there in landlocked Texas. He was doing a considerable amount of writing at this time, and the west coast experience is apparent on such surf and turf opuses as *Highway 101*, *Hangin' Ten*, and *Winter Surfin'* (possibly an early version of *King Of The Beach*) none of which, in addition to dozens of other handwritten songs, were ever committed to tape. The great, rockin' *Bodine* did make it to tape, as did the superb Holly-ish *Pamela* and *Angel Face* and *Jenny Lee as well*, but one can only imagine what songs like *What A Weekend, Don't Call A Girl A Broad, Sugar Baby, First Choice, Goodie Goodie Girl,* and *Get Out Of Bed, Teenage Loafer* might have sounded like. For certain, Bobby had his fingers on the pulse of young America, alternating attitudes between Holly and Cochran.

The band played to a motley crew at the venerable beachside Hermosa Biltmore Hotel, which Randy recalls as having an enthusiastic audience of 'old people and bums'. They also stomped successfully at a battle of the bands at the Rendezvous Ballroom, some forty miles south in Balboa. There they witnessed the King of the Surf Guitar, Dick Dale, with his Del-Tones, packing the joint with gremmies and surfers alike in hyped up swarms. This was a perfect world come to life to Bobby, a place he honestly believed he might replicate for the kids back home—a true teen club, just what El Paso needed, a hangout with loud music and no squares allowed. He couldn't wait to get back home to put the plan into action, and to crank up the reverb tank full-tilt.

Everything did go full-tilt (and then some) when the guys got home. Bobby had composed his surf opus *Stringer* on the beach in Balboa, and as soon as the guys returned to El Paso, they laid it to tape, along with the Cochran-style *Saturday Night*, and including a pair of Buddy-Holly-via-Johnny Fortune style ballads *You Made Me Cry My Love* and *Only For You*. Bobby immediately sent demos around, this time hitting labels in New York and Nashville. Still following in the footprints of his hero Buddy Holly, Bobby made a point to contact Paul Cohen, the Music City kingpin who had signed Buddy at Decca. Fifty-five year old Cohen must have heard something interesting in Bobby's Holly-fied Yucca releases, rocking Eastwood sides and the batch of new demos that he'd brought along as he tried quickly to sign Bobby, promising a 45 release before the end of the year. Bobby was thrilled to have a major Nashville producer behind him, and looked forward to the day that his Todd record could go national. Cohen paired the Eddie Cochran-styled *Saturday Night* with Bobby's quintessential surf instrumental, *Stringer*, soaked and stoked, and ramcharged with attitude. *Stringer* and Robby and the Robbins' *Surfer's Life* are sandwiched together on the Todd label between the Five Royales and Shy Guy Douglas. Surf and turf, and hold the mayo!

Meanwhile, there was minor chaos at Eastwood. Beat boy Jimmy Wagnon was due back in class after Labor Day, and Northwest import Larry Thompson, the only viable local trapster who could ever really keep up with Bobby, was quickly tapped for tubs for the newly hatched Fanatics.

"I was standing out on the street, minding by own business, when Bobby walked up to me and said, 'Hey, you wanna be in my band?' says Larry, and I said, 'Aw, okay, 'cause I had just got out of the Service and was looking to have fun. That's how I got with them. Bobby had seen me play before. He and I would do a solo together. We'd do *Wipe Out* or some stupid thing. He had the guitar and he'd turn around and grab some sticks and he'd bang on part of the drums and I had a part and we'd have a drum solo together. Randy was always in the band. We may have moved guitar players around but Randy and I were the only rhythm section while I was in the band. My drums were pink champagne Ludwigs, very nice. We were on TV on *Crosno's Hop* and we played at Crosno's club too, the Green Frog. It was always packed when we played there."

I FOUGHT THE LAW

Larry was also responsible for the band name. "I came up with the name the Frantics," says Larry. "It was a name out of Seattle. They had kinda split up in '63, got different members and stuff. So, we became the Southwest Frantics, and that was the name of the band. Bobby went out and got a banner made and it came back with the name the *Fanatics* on it. Bobby was mad that they made a mistake on the sign, but it was a big sign, so we changed the name of the band to the Fanatics."

"I had gone into the military when I was seventeen, but I had been in a band before that. The first band I was ever in was an all Black band, in fact those guys are still good friends of mine. We were called the Kingsmen. This was before *those* Kingsmen. Jerry Miller joined them after I went into the military. In my day the band was me, J.D. Roberts, L.J. Roberts, R. Cook and a guy named Storing. Then after I left, there was a guy named Johnny Moore who was with the group. And Johnny Moore's brother was Bobby Moore. Now, Bobby Moore changed his name to Ahmad Rashad when he became famous in the NFL as a wide receiver and later as a sportscaster. We all went to school together and I guess they needed a drummer. I was playing drums before I even had a set of drums, so I had to borrow drums from a guy named Tom Ewing. I didn't know anything about 'em, but I was in the high school band, but I just learned the beat and started playing with 'em. The Wailers were all my buddies. That's what inspired me. Mike Burk who's the drummer of the Wailers is the reason I play drums. Rich Dangel was with the Wailers, and he quit the them and joined the band that we had after we quit Bobby Fuller, the Rooks. And we ended up going back to El Paso, and Rich played with us down at the Little Dipper and all that stuff. But if you notice on some of Bobby's stuff, he recorded a couple of those Dangel tunes, like *Shanghied*. Dangel was just a killer guitar player."

I FOUGHT THE LAW

The Tacoma trapster had lured young guitarist extraordinaire Jerry Miller out of the Searchers, a band that included Jerry plus three members of the future Sonics—Rob Lind, Bob Bennett, and Jerry Roslie) up in Washington State to blast with his new El Paso band. Jerry was pals with Larry, and accepted the invitation to come stay with the Fullers and see what might work out. He arrived with the hard blues slam that Northwest guitarists fed upon, and he would, in turn, export the raunchy rabble blues of Long John Hunter and Little Joe Washington back to Tacoma, unintentionally cross pollinating NW with SW, merging two diverse musical worlds into a confident hybrid, his unique signature style. With Jerry, the group played regionally as far as Midland and Odessa. Jerry recalls that during his short sojourn in the Fanatics, work never ceased. The group was constantly rehearsing new material, working out for live appearances and recordings as well. But ultimately, Jerry felt like a fish out of water in the sunny suburban climes, and unused to being told what to play and how fast to play it. At the time, Bobby had made records that had entered and climbed the local hit parade, had worked with Norman Petty (big stuff to beat-crazed teenage Holly-heads) while Jerry had never recorded. Despite the promise of imminent records, possibly on a big time Nashville label, Jerry Miller answered the call back to his Northwest stomping grounds in October '63. He joined up with the spectacular Incredible Kings, eventually reigning supreme with Moby Grape as one of the most respected guitar players of all time. Jerry's early prowess is fearsomely evident on his first 1964 recordings with the Incredible Kings and with The Elegants, his friend Roger Freiheit's legendary NW garage combo—but not before trying to lure his Tacoma bandmate Rob Lind down to El Paso to blast a sax in Bobby's band.

"One night Jerry Miller called me on the telephone and asked me to come down to El Paso to play with him and Bobby," says Rob. "My dad asked, who's on the phone and I said 'it's Jerry Miller, Dad, and he wants me to go to El Paso to play with Bobby Fuller.' 'You're not going anywhere,' says Dad. And there ended my five minute fantastic dream of going to Texas to play with Bobby Fuller!"

"Jerry and I went to school together," says Larry. "We were from the same neighborhood and grew up in Coleman together. Never in the same class, but neighborhood kids. He was more of a bluesy kind of guy, it wasn't quite the thing for Bobby when you came down to it. He was a good guitar player but it wasn't his thing. The Fantics was just Bobby, me and Randy and then we brought Jerry down. I don't remember anybody else bein' in the band early on, including Jim. There wasn't another guitar player ever that I can remember."

Iowa guitar blaster Billy Webb was drafted into Jerry's newly-vacated spot in the Fanatics just as the pot was about to boil, and fortunately he came bearing a Fender guitar, which had been a bone of contention for Bobby with both Jim Reese and Jerry Miller, who were loyal to Gretsch guitars. The band was now decked out completely in almighty Fenders, and was ready to roar.

Bobby had secured a vacant venue at Hondo Village Shopping Center, and with the support of his parents, signed a lease for BOBBY FULLER'S TEEN RENDEZVOUS, a no-booze teen club where the Fanatics would be the house band. A stage was built, their Altec sound system was installed, membership cards were printed, decorations were purchased. The $1,000 bank loan for the new business came through the week President Kennedy was assassinated. The impact of JFK's murder was spiritually devastating, and for young and old, the world was forever changed. Everyone of age remembers where they were on Nov. 22, 1963—certainly, no one was in the mood to romp and stomp in Texas, the state where the deed was done.

"I remember exactly where I was when it happened," says Larry. "I remember exactly what I was doing. I was eating a Milk Bone dog biscuit. Yup, a Milk Bone. I had bought a little poodle for my mother and I was gonna send it to her. I was eating one of those biscuits when Kennedy got shot. The little dog was there with me and I looked at the TV and I had a Milk Bone in my hand. So that's where I was when that happened. So if we want to set a stage, we have to go from Kennedy's death. Everything happened after that day."

It took determination, psychology, and pure grit to rehearse new material and get the teen club up and running while the nation was under the black cloud of the death in Texas, but sure enough, by Monday, December 23, the doors flew back at the Bobby Fuller's Teen Rendezvous, with the Fanatics stomping through ten days in a row (including Christmas Eve and Christmas Day night), culminating in a massive New Years Eve blowout. Finally, El Paso had its own teen club, complete with membership cards, regular dance contests and its own cop to keep out the boring over 21's.

CHAPTER EIGHT

STRINGER
Whitewash and the destiny factor in
the land of teenage plenty,
winning and losing and chasing a dream.

Beginning January 1, 1964, the Fanatics would play two to four nights a week at the Rendezvous, with the remaining days filled in by local combos like Bill Taylor and the Sherwoods, who boasted the third and last release on Bobby's Eastwood label, after the Chancellors disc. Bobby changed the name of his label to the Saxonesque *Exeter,* continuing the numbering system and colors and boasting Old English lettering. The first Exeter release was the keg-tapping *Wine, Wine, Wine,* which was backed with the world class teen opus *King Of The Beach*—a surf vocal anthem that rivals the Trashmen's *King Of The Surf.* Bobby paid a promotion company two hundred dollars to push the single, pressing 500 promo DJ copies for distribution to radio stations. This ferocious single shows off all of the Holly/Valens/Cochran/Dale lessons fully osmosed. The February 1964 release charted in March on KELP's Fab Forty and the stock copy pressing of 476 copies sold out quickly.

The Rendezvous was a teenage heaven—everything about it was unique, including the do-it-yourself decor. Randy de-

I FOUGHT THE LAW

scribes the scene: "We put up these big parachutes that we got from the supply sergeant, Bruce Gravy. He was like the guy you'd see in that movie *No Time For Sergeants*. We got a drag chute from a jet, it's the one that slows the jet down, real bright yellow. We put that up on one side of the teen club and spread out the complete thing. Then we took the other silk net. It was beautiful, white, kind of transparent, and we put it up on the other side, put it up, stapled it up and it hung down just like if you were falling from the sky. And if it had ever caught fire, that would've been a bad thing, now that I look back. You know, light shining through that parachute, it was like a big old balloon that was lit up. It was as good as psychedelic lighting and in its own way it was artistically unique. And I wish that we had pictures of it, somebody has to have pictures of the parachutes in that club. Luckily, nobody smoked inside. People smoked outside, though. Teenagers smoked young in this town, 'cause all their fathers and mothers were from the days of Humphrey Bogart and all those heavy smokers, you know. El Paso was a

Bobby in his home studio, 1964, the night they cut I Fought The Law

smokers paradise."

On non-Rendezvous nights, the Fanatics rehearsed, recorded in Bobby's garage studio, and filled in nights playing at other teen dances, 21+ clubs, bowling alleys, shopping centers, proms, military bases, and social events within a two hundred mile radius of El Paso, lugging their Altec A-7 state of the art public address system along in their beloved Chevrolet Corvair Greenbrier van, with a trailer in tow. Their shows were legendary events in the landlocked Southwest, with the combo serving up reverb-drenched surf instrumentals and wild romps on Holly, Cochran, and Presley material between showcasing their original recorded tunes and great new originals as well.

"I lived at Bobby's house," says Larry Thompson, "I had a room down the hall. So you know, we were ready to roll any time of day or night, because we had access to the studio any time Bobby wanted to go. Most of the Album Avenue recordings were just Bobby, Randy and I, with Bobby playing all the guitar parts. I play drums on *Stringer*, I play drums on *Saturday Night*, I play drums on the original version of *I Fought The Law*. We played music everywhere, all the time. I remember us playing up on the roof of that travel center at Bassett Shopping Center, and at the Little Dipper Lounge—it's a church now. That bowling alley lounge was a pretty new and great place at the time. They had the best tacos in the *world*, soft tacos that were just incredible. I worked there with Joe Richie, and I worked there with Bobby. The teen club was on the rough side of town and they'd get fights and stuff. It was just a normal teenage thing. Yeah, that was always goin' on there. The Dipper place was always packed. I mean it was just, it was like, *nuts*. For me it was like, for a guy out of the service and going with Bobby right after that, it was like, 'wow, this must be what it's really like just to be in a band.' You know?"

Mike Ciccarelli rates Bobby's sidemen. "Larry was very energetic, with a high communication level, an incredible drummer—he was an *incredible* drummer. But Bobby, he knew exactly what he wanted, so he didn't deal with polished musicians, he dealt with guys that had strong backbeat. Dewayne fit that mold and Dalton was your classic Texas rockabilly. Willy Wilson was another one. Bobby Taylor wasn't too shabby, either. He played a lot of different instruments, but he wasn't quite as polished as Dalton or Willy. When Bobby Fuller played drums, I went over to the house and he just wanted to talk about music. He sat down at the piano, played for about five or ten minutes. Went over and said, 'You know, while I was gone, I learned how to play the saxophone.' And I'm saying, 'Yeah, right. How the hell can you learn to play a saxophone in five months?' He picked up the sax and did everything you possibly could do on a saxophone in two or three minutes. So it was at this point it was like, 'Oh Jesus! This guy is not normal. He's not normal!' If he wanted to, he could play the most intricate jazz passages, and it would be thirty years outta their time, but he didn't. He went into heavy back beat rock and roll, which definitely was the frontier. If the Beatles hadn't have happened, his music would've been ten times what it was. Oh yeah, I went to a lot of dances at the Rendezvous. They were insane. It was always a riot waiting to happen, always, and the riot was driven by the music. There was always gonna be a fight, and the reason there was a fight was because the music was so adrenaline-charged. That was the problem. Everybody stands around looking' at the other guy, thinking, 'what's *their* problem?' Well, if you stand there and listen to *Thunder* and you're seventeen years old... okay, so you know what I mean. So the atmosphere was always super-charged. But Fuller was very careful where he played, because he never overexposed himself. When he showed up, it was like a steamroller. Every time he played, it was incredible songs, everything was perfectly polished, everything was perfect. He never played a dead gig in his life. He always knew where to play, when to play it and never to overplay it. So I mean, everyone in the town is like, 'Is he gonna make it?' It's not a matter of if, it's *when*. He's gotta get the hell outta here. It was like, man, what's this guy still doing here? It was a destiny factor in this town, it was like man, this guy's unbelievable. You had to go to the west coast. You had to. El Paso was dead. Houston, Dallas, Austin, Fort Worth, basically that was it. A few things happening in San Antonio, but not much. Sunny and the Sunliners, nothing but noisy impact. El Paso had some blazing impact of its own, but it's because of that conversion. Why did that happen? Because it's geographically disjointed. It's six hundred miles to the other side of the state. It's a dot in the middle of nowhere. On the Rand McNally maps, it used to be colored as the least densest populated area in the United States. You know, they do the shading, browns and greens and reds? This is one region that it was in the middle of a goddamn Sahara Desert. But it's another reason that man that place was hotter than a match, 'cause he was all that was happening in this entire area."

The Fanatics were unstoppable—ready to conquer the scene, which is precisely what they did. Billy Webb, who had come in on guitar after Jerry Miller returned to the Pacific Northwest, had been playing in bands since 1958 in Primghar, Iowa about fifty miles from Clear Lake, where Buddy Holly played his last show.

"Donnie Rohrs taught me how to play guitar chords and some licks," says Billy, speaking of the Iowa's country and western legend. "We had the Black Cats, and the Idlers, and a

I FOUGHT THE LAW

couple of other groups, and we played all around Iowa—Lake Okoboji, Storm Lake, Sioux City. The joints we played were all dance halls, no bars at that time, at all. I went to California in 1962 and we got busted for being too young at a casino that we were playing in, so we ended up in Albuquerque where Donnie Rohrs went with another band. We had met Dewayne Quirico there, who was just starting on drums. He was a natural. I took Dewayne with me when I went down to Santa Rosa, New Mexico to play. We were playing for exotic dancers and the bar crowd there. I met Bobby and Randy's cousin at that club and he told me I should call Bobby 'cause he was looking for a guitar player, so I did, and they said come on down. I hopped on a train and took off for El Paso. Bobby and Randy picked me up at the station. I had some tapes that I had cut in California and they put them on in the studio and heard me play guitar and I got the job. I had met James Burton and Glen Campbell in California and I tried to copy the way they played. They were the guitar players I looked up to at the time, as well as Bobby Birdsong, a picker from Kansas. El Paso was a cool town back then. It was still kind of the Old West when I got there. I got to play with a lot of good pickers. Bobby was one of them. He showed me a lot of cool things on the guitar. Big Sonny Farlow was a great player, and so was Joe Richie, and Joe Johnson, and Long John Hunter, whose drummer Miguel was... wow! I remember one time we had a jam session at the Rendezvous, and Charlie Daniels came and played guitar and jammed with us. Also there was a guy named Chicken down there who was great—he became a cop in El Paso. I used to go sit in with him at the Green Frog, Steve Crosno's club on Pershing between Piedras and Copia. While I was with Bobby, we recorded a lot of songs including *Pamela, King Of The Beach, Never To Be Forgotten, Nervous Breakdown,* and *Not Fade Away.* That time was a part of my life I will never forget. Bobby and I never had words and I always respected him."

Larry recalls life in the Fanatics, "Mickey Davis was a guy I was in the military with, and when I got out of the service, I was living in a house by the teen club. Well, Mickey had left town and then turns back up, this little short guy with a big suitcase full of money. And he said he'd won it in Las Vegas. So he bought, I think, Randy and Bobby some clothes, and he paid off my drums, and he did all this nice stuff. And then one night, we're sittin' there having a drink, just him and I, and then the story comes out. Him and his brother had pulled an armed robbery on a bank in Phoenix. He was still on the lam. I couldn't believe that, and figured he was full of hot air. And so, uh, he lived with us a little while, and then he bought a Corvette. Randy could tell you all this stuff, guitars and stuff he bought. And, uh, the FBI shows up at the club, looks for him at my house and they go through all the garbage. Mickey had split out of town that day, I guess he got some wind of how they were gonna be in town. They show up at the teen club, you know, they swarm in there in the FBI cars and all that and talked to everybody there, and we didn't know where the guy was. Apparently they caught him on the way out of town, holed up in a bathroom at a gas station, helicopters and everything. And that's the last time we ever saw him."

"There was always a fight around the corner in El Paso at that time," he continues. "One time, Donnie Rohrs came to visit Billy from Iowa and we ended up across the border with

> THE RENDEZVOUS
> presents Bobby Vee
> Sat. June 27, 1964
> 8:00 - 12:00 p. m.
>
> Advance tickets $ 2.00 per person

Randy Fuller. We got in a hell of a fight and got dragged to jail by the Federales. They took our watches and rings and money and cut us loose. But they didn't get it all 'cause we kept most of our money in our boots. It was cool living at the Fuller house with Bobby and his folks. Loraine was a great cook and all that stuff. And Randy, well, he was married, so he was off somewhere else so I had his room. It felt great. I had I started bringin' girls home to the Fullers' house and, it was getting kind of weird with Loraine. Mary Ann, Randy's wife at the time, well, her grandmother had her own house down in south El Paso or somewhere down there, so I left and rented a room from her. I kinda blew it with Mrs. Fuller."

Running the teen club kept Bobby moving, yet he squeezed himself into his home studio at every opportunity. He showcased local combo the Sherwoods at the Rendezvous after his release of their *Tickler/Black Out* (Exeter 45-123), which he had recorded and produced, complete with backwash and breakwater surf sounds, plus laughter and yelling—everything a discerning audiophile might demand from the hi-fi experience. Throughout the fall of '63 and until the end of summer '64, he kept his own band playing, rehearsing, and recording at a furious pace. A look at Fanatics set lists for this period show literally hundreds of cover songs, including *Kuk, I Got A Woman, Church Key, Red Cadillac And A Black Moustache, Move On Down The Line, Nadine*—even Eddie Cochran's *Drive In Show*, Roy Orbison's *Rockhouse* and Elvis' *Baby I Don't Care*. By this time, Bobby had also moved from the audience to the stage at Long John's shows and was actually playing guitar with him on occasion, although he left the rafter-hanging acrobatics to Long John.

Meanwhile, back at the Rendezvous, Rick Stone relates, "Things were wild—totally wild! I mean I wasn't there because

I FOUGHT THE LAW

we had moved up to Dallas, but I heard from everybody back home. Northeast El Paso could get pretty rough, believe me! GI's on leave and crazy kids—the press and police started getting on Bobby's back saying they'd throw everybody out of the club if there were any more fights, 'cause that was always going on. One night these two guys started going at it right in front of the stage so Randy just took off his bass in the middle of a song and whacked this one guy right in the back of the head and of course the guy went out cold! Randy just put his bass back on and kept playing like nothing had happened! See, Randy wasn't afraid of anybody. A few years earlier when we were still in high school, I remember Bobby and Randy were playing at some bowling alley and Randy was having this big argument with some girl during a break, really going at it. This GI comes up and tells Randy, who was only like seventeen, 'Hey, man, leave that girl alone,' so Randy tells him to get lost and the guy keeps bothering him, so Randy goes POW! Knocked the guy

The Fanatics! Larry Thompson, Randy Fuller, Bobby Fuller, Billy Webb

I FOUGHT THE LAW

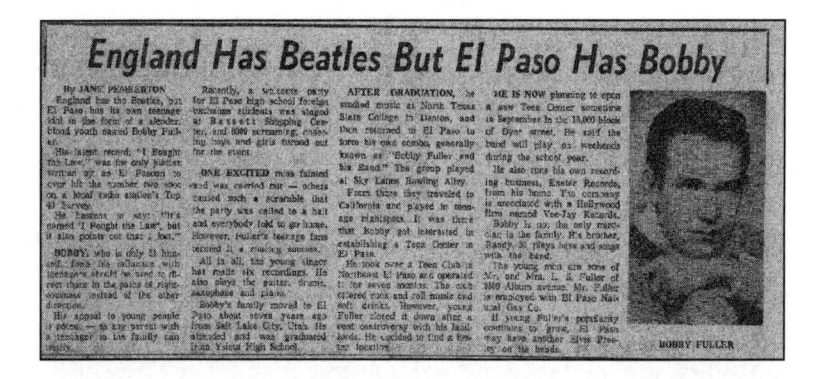

England Has Beatles But El Paso Has Bobby

right through a plate glass window and the guy nearly bleeds to death!"

The aftermath recalled by Rick is disputed by Randell. Rick recalled, "So the next day we're at school at band practice, you know with the school band. Randy's playing trombone and I'm on trumpet and Bobby's on drums and in walk two cops who go 'DO YOU HAVE RANDELL FULLER HERE?' And Randy just slid right down behind that music stand but they saw him and the band director says, real cool and calm like, 'Randell Fuller, please come down here now,' and poor Randell had to get up and go get himself taken away by the cops!"

Randell insists that Rick has two incidents confused, that he was out of school by the time the described arrest occurred. In fact, says Randell, the arrest occurred at Skylanes Bowling Alley.

"Randell was always more of an extrovert than Bobby," added Rick. "He was always getting in fights and making homemade bombs and all, sort of a daredevil. I mean, the Fuller brothers were really very close even though they were different when it came to personality. Both of them were into cars. Randell got this '59 Corvette cheap when it was about a year old 'cause the owner had let the engine go. One night the cops started chasin' him and Bobby for speeding. Well, Randy and Bobby sped up 'til they got way ahead of the cops and then Randell dropped Bobby off in front of their house and Bob ran in and Randy peeled back out again with the cops chasin' him. Meanwhile, Bobby went and opened the garage door while Randy ripped around the block and tore up their street with his headlights off and ripped right up the driveway and into the garage. Bob slammed the garage door down and those cops went around the neighborhood all night with the siren on!"

Local combos filled in the gaps between Fanatics shows at the Rendezvous, but Bobby took another big step by booking nationally known Buddy Holly acolyte, Liberty artist Bobby Vee, for a June 27 show at the club. The event was a major risk. Vee's fee was one thousand dollars, and with advertising, printed tickets, and general gussying up of the premises, Bobby was hoping to break even. But by summer of '64, the British invasion had the music biz in a spin. Not only had the Beatles Sullivanized the entire pimple population, but the Rolling Stones had just cracked things wide open with the wildest TV appearance ever courtesy Dean Martin on *Hollywood Palace* which had aired on June 14. Bobby Vee was straight off the opening slot on the Stones tour and there can be little speculation that he represented exactly what the Stones were *not*. The Rendezvous show did not break even—far from it. The Fanatics kept barreling ahead, but not for long.

"In about late summer '64, Billy and I quit," said Larry. "Bobby was working us at union scale, like twenty-six bucks a week, and there was this another group, with Joe Richie, working six nights a week and after-hours and, we had like a chance to make a hundred and twenty-five dollars a week. And, you know, young and foolish and all that kind of stuff, but that was what it was. I can't think of any other reason other than that, just that the money was there. Bobby never sat down and talked with us about the band, and if he had, maybe I would have stayed. He never sat down and let it out, you know, kind of what his plans were, never said a word about goin' to California. If he'd done that, it might've been a different thing. He just sort of kept things to himself. And so, to me, it looked like a dead end road, you know? You're playin' there, you know, okay, so we make twenty-six bucks a week forever. It was never, 'Hey, hang in there, we're gonna make more money if we just do this and that.' He never talked, nothin'. So we never really knew anything."

"Joe Richie offered us a lot of money," says Billy Webb, "So we flipped a coin as to who was gonna have to tell Bobby we were quittin' and I won, so Larry had to call him. Bobby answered the phone and Larry said, 'is your mother there?' He told Bobby's *mother* that we were going to quit. To this day I could never figure out why he didn't just tell Bobby! Bobby had started working on *She's My Girl*, a new original that was popular with the kids at the club. It was brother Randy who suggested they record Cricket Sonny Curtis' composition *I Fought The Law*. Randy has joked that the song seemed to have personal meaning to him, considering his run-ins with overbearing local police officers.

Rick Stone recalled, "I was at a recording session of *I Fought The Law*. Bobby set up everything, ran the whole show, did all the work setting up and running things. He had to run through the den, then through the garage and into the storage room, which was his control booth. He had two Ampex machines in there and he'd built some cubicles out of chicken wire and burlap just before that session, so he was really going for a home version of a real recording studio at that point. I got over to his place about 9:30 and Bobby was still working on it at 4:30. It was pretty wild. I remember Randy tellin' him

I FOUGHT THE LAW

to 'kiss my butt' at one point, but I guess Bobby realized all the while that it was all Randell's idea to do the song."

Jim Gallomore was adamant in his surprising recollection of meeting members of the Standells in El Paso. "The last time I was at the Fuller house was in the summer of '64 just before I went overseas to Germany with the USAF. The Standells were there and wanted to do some recording, but Bobby said he was having technical difficulties with some of the equipment. Funny about the things we remember with such clarity, because I clearly remember Bobby selling the Standells drummer a pair of drumsticks for fifty cents." Bobby could have met Dick Dodd a year earlier in Hermosa Beach, and most likely was aware of the Standells records on Liberty, and also their *Live at PJ's* album. He would certainly follow a similar flight pattern in California.

Bobby talked Jim Reese and Dalton Powell into returning to the fold with the promise of two imminent Exeter releases and improved paychecks (Bobby would no longer take his share in order to make this happen). The pair came in just in time for the July 4th record release bash for Exeter 124, a top teener called *She's My Girl* backed with what would become their calling card, *I Fought The Law*. Seven hundred copies of the RCA custom pressing on Exeter started making noise in the region. Coupled with two subsequent pressings totaling twenty-four hundred records, the sales brought spirits up considerably, but not for long.

Following *I Fought The Law* was Exeter 125, a Fuller production for a local band called the Pawns, comprised of leader David Hayes, plus Jack Duncan on bass, and Gary Davis on drums. Gary had just replaced Randy's old sidekick Jimmy Wagnon on the traps. Both sides of the single, *The Pawn* and *South Bay*, are intense, moody instrumentals. *The Pawn* is actually the Astronauts' *Movin'*, thanks to band member roots in Colorado, where from the Astronauts hailed. The Pawns would return on Exeter 127 as The Pawns *Lonely* b/w David Hayes *Meet Me Here*.

July 18, 1964, would mark the last night for the Rendezvous—after seventy-six nights of teenage heaven, Bobby, Randy, Jim and Dalton unknowingly played their last blast there. The club got hit with a distress warrant the following day, and then by a lawsuit. Padlocked, and rent due, the Rendezvous was soon in arrears, but the records kept on coming from the garage studio on Album Avenue. Bobby's latest recording stars the Pawns won the Battle of the Bands contest at Bassett Center the week of August 21, on the heels of their Exeter release. Bobby immediately hooked the guys up at a club in Farmington, where

I FOUGHT THE LAW

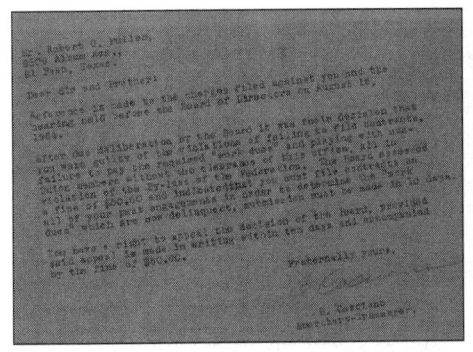

Jack and Gary were soon snagged for a Durango, Colorado group called the Lords Of London with promises of big money and Hollywood. The Lords would end up recording a snarling version of an Arthur Lee and Johnny Echols demo called *Stay Away*—twice, and with different lead singers and a change in band names. With band name the Bundys, *Stay Away* appeared several months later on the Tony Sepe/Marty Brooks/Bob Krasnow owned Domain label. As the Lords of London, it was the sole foal of Domain's Shot Records subsidiary. Both versions are excellent, both produced by Sepe/Brooks. Domain was distributed by Laurie subsidiary Rust. How exactly anyone ever got to hear that demo, which would remained undiscovered and unreleased until 2006, is anyone's guess, but it is likely that it landed either on Bob Keene's desk at Maravilla (and was spotted by Barry White, who would become Tony Sepe's songwriting partner) or on Buck Ram's desk at Personality Productions, as the demo was recorded with Ram. Arthur and Johnny, who can be heard, with bandmates Larry Taylor and Henry Vestine (both who would go on to Canned Heat), on Del-Fi subsidiary Selma with their remarkable ode *Luci Baines*, aimed at President Johnson's teenage daughter, can also be credited with the first release on Mustang Records. As the Surfettes, they backed Carol Connors on *Sammy The*

I FOUGHT THE LAW

Sidewalk Surfer, which boasted an excellent instrumental flip called *Blue Surf*. The fact that the Surfettes were the first act on Mustang deflates the statement that Bob Keene made to Bobby and the band, that being that he had created the label for Bobby Fuller. That plainly was not the case.

The chapter on Bobby's Exeter label was about to close. In total, he had issued nine singles on Exeter and Eastwood, as well as a 1964 album by a folk rock trio called Los Paisanos. The back of the LP states the facts, and then some, "Mr. Bob Fuller of the Exeter Record Company, 9509 Album Avenue, El Paso, Texas produced and directed this recording. Mr. Fuller, an outstanding popular vocalist in his own right, composes, sings and records original material. Los Paisanos are indebted to Mr. Fuller for his able direction and sound engineering. A Fuller Production." Although Los Paisanos did not fully represent the rock and roll sound of Bobby Fuller—and truth be told, the group had paid for the recording and manufacture of the album—the fact that a twelve inch record had sprung from the loins of the tiny garage studio on Album Avenue must have opened up a world of ideas for Bobby.

Bobby booked steady local shows for the Fanatics through

LEFT: *Randy and fans;*
RIGHT: *The Fanatics are on top!*

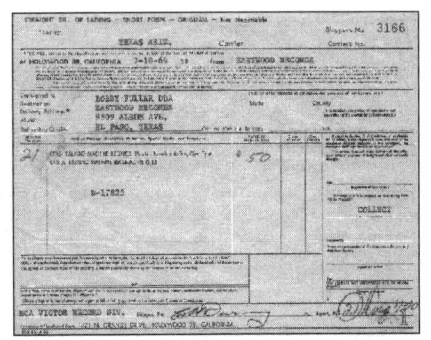

Halloween of 1964. It was traumatic for all of them to step down from ruling the scene from their own secure teen club roost, but they forged ahead, roadtripping to Carlsbad and Farmington, and playing locally at the Johnny Fairchild's Golden Key Club. Change was in the air, and one of the changes was a new man on the traps—Dewayne Quirico was about to replace Dalton Powell.

"I had been playing with Billy Webb in Santa Rosa, New Mexico, back before he joined the Fanatics. He heard that Bobby Fuller was looking for a guitar player and he took off for El Paso. I just stayed behind and hooked up with other bands and played the same circuit. It was a long while after that, when I was in Santa Fe to see Donny Rohrs, that Billy turned up there, having quit Bobby, and he says, 'You know, you need to go to El Paso, Bobby's looking for a drummer.' So we pile my drums in this guy Jack Brigshaw's Mustang and head for El Paso. And we get into town and we go to eat at a Red Rooster Drive-In. And there's Randy Fuller sittin' in this car with some guy. I get outta Jack's car and walk over toward Randy and he goes, 'I hear you wanna be in our band.' Now, I had no idea he even knew I was coming, which is weird. So he sticks a bottle of Jack Daniels out in front of me. 'Here, take a drink.' And I didn't drink, but I said, 'Okay, I'll take drink.' So then the next day, we rehearsed—well, you know, the audition was set up and we did four songs at Bobby and Randy's home. And uh, at about the four songs, Bobby stopped our audition and he called me into the kitchen and he said, 'I see you have potential, and I like the way you play. Would you go to California and play what I want you to play on my songs?' And I said, 'Do we leave right now?' And he said, 'soon,' and that's how that happened."

The first night that Dewayne Quirico replaced Dalton Powell was Thursday, September 24 at the Golden Key, with Mike Ciccarelli sitting in for Randy on that date, as Randy was recuperating from tonsil surgery. He was back in action for their big gig performing for the Prez the following day.

"One of the last shows we ever did in El Paso was at the airport when LBJ came to meet with the president of Mexico," recalls Randy of the visit by President Lyndon Johnson on September 25. "I can't recall how we got the gig. I just had my tonsils out a couple days earlier and when LBJ arrived and was getting off the plane, we started playing *She Loves You* by the Beatles and went into 'We love you LBJ' instead 'She loves you yeah, yeah, yeah' and every one started singing with us. Maybe his teenage daughter Luci was along and they thought she'd like some rock and roll. I wasn't singing because of my throat, and Bobby kept telling me to sing so I forced it and after the gig I had to go back to the hospital because I started hemor-

LEFT: *Randy meets the audience;*
RIGHT: *Christmas 1962*

I FOUGHT THE LAW

rhaging. The was the last time I went out for politics!"

That same day, Bobby took delivery of the the RCA lacquers for his next Exeter record, *Fool Of Love/Shakedown*.

Ray Ruff of Checkmate Productions, one of the biggest talent bookers in the Southwest, had expressed serious interest in booking the Fanatics. "I've heard a lot of good compliments about you," wrote Ruff to Bobby, "We have syndicated all the bands on KOMA (radio) and we can get you spots and probably work a deal to book you straight through next summer."

Bobby stalled on the offer, as he had his own bookings now to take the band through Thanksgiving. In October, with new basher Dewayne Quirico in tow, the band played dances at the Elks Club in Carlsbad, as well as the Women's Club there, and the Carlsbad Armory. There were also gigs at Biggs Army Airfield and Fort Bliss, a club called the Plantation, and on October 17, a date with the Crickets at the Golden Key. On October 23, the guys drove to Carlsbad again to play the Women's Club dance. They parked the Corvair Greenbrier van and went down the street to grab a bite, only to return to find the van emptied of most of their gear. Dewayne's beautiful gold sparkle Ludwig tom toms were gone, as well as their Fender Showman amps, reverb units and guitars (and, according to the police report, a chromatic harmonica and a bag of guitar cords).

Jim Reese recalls, "When all of our guitars and amps were stolen, we had to go out and buy equipment on the spot and the shop we went to carried nothing but Fender guitars. Bobby of course was happy that I had to get one. As luck, if you want to call it that, would have it, my new Fender was stolen soon after that and I went right out and got a Gibson for myself. It bothered Bobby. He had a one-track mind and there was no getting around it. He loved Fender guitars."

The loss was another huge setback for Bobby—first the teen club, now all the equipment, most of which had been purchased on credit, and was being paid off in weekly installments. Back in El Paso, Bobby found a dream location for a new club just a couple of miles away from the old Rendezvous, on Dyer Street, a big building with a loading dock and plenty of open dance floor space. His dream to reopen with a new place would never came to be. Lawson and Loraine, afraid of new and bigger trouble, refused to co-sign for another loan for a new club. A series of incidents both legal and personal, as well as the band member switches, all seemed to suggest a change of venue. "We had a going away party the night before we left," remembers Dewayne. "We rented this place where there where these Mexicans, the Starlighters, were playin' upstairs, and we played in the downstairs area. The next morning, we all took off for California in Mrs. Fuller's car."

In retrospect, there were a few additional reasons that the Fanatics headed out of town. In August the El Paso Federation of Musicians had filed charges against Bobby for "violations of failing to file contracts, failure to pay the required work dues and playing with non-Union members without clearance." There had also been a near-miss at the teen club that had involved firearms.

"Okay," says Randy, "I did hit that guy with the bass, you know. And then when some guys came in on Sunday, I'd kicked their asses, too, because they were hanging around the northeast area out there, gang-wise, you know, a little gang. They came into the club on that Sunday when Bobby and I were cleaning up. One of 'em was swingin' a sawed off baseball bat. I put up a scuffle with 'em and got clobbered on my right arm and I ran in and got the .22 outta the office and we chased 'em out the door with the rifle. Bobby had unloaded and I then when I pulled the chamber back to cock and fire, nothing went off. Luckily for me, 'cause I would probably have shot the bastard, you know? Anyway, that was one week, and there's other reasons too. The owners wanted more rent, they maybe just wanted us out of there. They were gonna up the rent and everything, and it was hard enough as it was. And at that point, we were gonna move out to that great big beautiful place out there on Dyer. A whole new building. It was like a big warehouse. And it was all concrete, and had a loading dock for trucks. It was huge and it would've been fantastic, but my dad wouldn't sign for it."

"There was a big front page article in the *Herald-Post* in September, 'England Has Beatles But El Paso Has Bobby' about how the new Teen Center was gonna open for the new school year. But it wasn't gonna happen, not without a loan and Dad wasn't gonna take the risk. That's when I just told Bobby, I said,

'Let's go to California, it's time, we gotta get out of here.' You know, so we went. And I'm not really sure if Bobby would've come out if hadn't really pushed it. I'm not really sure about it, you know. I don't know. 'Cause he would've had that teen club goin' and it would've been getting his name around. Southwest king and stuff. I'm not really sure if he really wanted to go, I just kept pushing him, 'cause I really wanted to go. I really did."

CHAPTER NINE

TEENAGE HEAVEN
Love and loss in the sand dunes,
and racing with the wind.

The Rendezvous was described by its denizens as a "teenage heaven". Cascading backlit pastel parachutes hovered over a bristling mob of underage rabble rousers. Suburban high schoolers and bordertown middle school kids and east side dropouts and Pachuco glue sniffers all mixed and moved at the Hondo Village teen club. A rent-a-cop dozed by the entrance with a big flashlight, oblivious to the drinking and fighting. She-devils with ratted coifs and white lipsick sidled up against lean boys in chinos and madras shirts. A firecracker or stink bomb would go off unannounced and all the girls would shriek and giggle. Everybody who was nobody was at the Rendezvous, and they were there to hear the band make some noise.

By spring of 1964, Bobby's sweetheart, Pamela (we have withheld surnames in this chapter for privacy reasons) was living with her family in Pecos, some two hundred miles east as the crow flies. They had relocated because of Pamela's fathers work. Bobby and Pam had met in 1962, and were engaged to be married a year later.

LEFT: *Bobby and fans at La Cave Pigalle;*
RIGHT: *Bobby's girl, Pamela*

Pamela remembers, "I met Bobby at a party at his house. I went with a friend. The parents weren't home. He came up and introduced himself and asked me if we could go out. I told him I needed to ask my parents. I had never dated. I was fourteen, he was eighteen years old. I went to school at Eastwood High School and Bobby would always play at the dances there. Couples used to wear matching shirts and my mom made some for us, that's how it was back then. We got pretty serious right away and got engaged. In 1963 my family moved to Pecos. He actually came and played at dances there. My dad was still traveling back to El Paso on business and we still had relatives there, and my dad came home one time and said he had heard rumors that Bobby was dating other girls. It went downhill after that. It was a long distance romance. We ended up breaking up in early '65. I sent him his ring back and I went off to college. He took the diamond out and put it into a pinkie ring for himself. By the summer of 1966, I was back in Pecos, working, getting ready to go back to school in the fall, and he came to see me. He came to visit in June. I was working days so he actually spent more time with my mother. At that time he asked me to go back to California with him. I told Bobby I couldn't, that I was in school. He said, 'well, you can go to school in California.' I told him I needed some time to think about it. And then we got the call from his mom. The hardest part was not really knowing what happened to him."

In 1964, with Pamela two hundred miles away, temptation took over at the rock and roll shows. One early summer evening, the Fullers were visited by the livid father of a pregnant fifteen year old named Mary. He claimed that Bobby had forced himself on his daughter at the Rendezvous. With a statutory rape charge just a phone call away, the Fullers agreed to an unnegotiable arrangement with Mary's father that traded funded confidence for the elimination of the "situation". The girl was sent to New Mexico for the duration of her pregnancy, returning alone to El Paso in early 1965. As far as neighbors and schoolmates knew, Mary had been away, visiting distant relatives. She soon met a new boy, married, and started a new family. Mary's son had been adopted at birth in New Mexico and would not learn of his natural parents until his birth mother tracked him down and went public with her story, decades later. John did have a chance to meet Loraine Fuller before her passing. He plays occasional guitar, and lives today in the Pacific Northwest.

At the same time of Mary's pregnancy in 1964, Bobby found himself again informed that he was about to be a father. Things were getting complicated for the 21 year old Bobby, who was still engaged to Pamela.

Suzie tells her story here for the first time.

"I went to Irvin High School—yes, with Sharon Tate," recalls Suzie. "I graduated in 1963. I used to hang out with the Fuller gang, even though I didn't know Bobby and Randy at the start. I met Googie Dirmeyer and Bobby Taylor at another teen club that was way out on the highway. Bobby Taylor was about 6'3, a redhead. Googie used to sing *Donna* to me. I remember going with a bunch of girls to the Rendezvous for the first time. We were standing by the side of the stage when the band were playing. The girls were all going, 'Randy's so cute! Look how cute Randy is!' Everybody was just gaga over Randy. Not one person mentioned Robert. When they took a break, they came over to us to talk to us. Robert talked to me and it was, 'Yeah, whatever'—it wasn't like love at first sight, like 'Oh God you're so cute!' or anything. I think that made him more interested because I didn't want anything to do with him. Most people remember the very first time they went out—what they wore, what they did, where they went, but I didn't really like him so I don't remember. I had no designs on him whatsoever. I thought he was kinda cute. But then we started seeing each other. He never came to my house. I always went to his house. I used to go to the bowling alley whenever they played and I always sat with Loraine and she always watched over me. Robert and I did silly stuff. We didn't go out to dinners and romantic bullshit. We were just homebodies. We either were at his house or my apartment or my best friend Sandy's.

We had a wreck in the Corvette one night. He was racing with another guy. We thought, 'Oh my God, our names will be in the paper tomorrow!' That was big news but the presses burned down that night and the paper didn't come out.

One night we were at a party and we were sitting back in the corner. He said, 'I got my ring back from Pam. I told her I had to get the diamond checked. I'm not giving it back to her.' I was so elated, so excited that he got the ring back. I was just beside myself. But then I found out later he did give it back to her. I spent a lot of time at the teen club. It was either me or

Loraine taking in the money at the front desk. I remember the day Bobby Vee came to the club. It was so funny—here we have a star coming to the teen club and they drive up in this old car, him and his wife, a cute little couple with their luggage and I thought, 'This is the star?'

I remember when Bobby's record was played on Bandstand. We were at Sandy's house making chicken fajita flautas. We were all sitting in the living room watching on TV. That was later. But Sandy's house was by the desert and we'd always go out there with blankets. We had a lot of sex. In the Corvette, at Bobby's house. I don't call him Bobby. I'm doing it now and it doesn't feel right. I always called him Robert or Rat Fink. Randy got mad and said, 'No, I'm Rat Fink!' All the time from when I was five months pregnant until she was born, I called my baby Mouse, because she was Rat Fink's baby.

I remember the night that I went to tell him I was pregnant. They were playing at the bowling alley. I told them at the door I was with the band. He was really glad to see me. When they were finished I said, 'Can we go somewhere and talk?' And he said, 'You want to go to a motel?' And I said, 'Yeah, I would.' I wanted some intermittent place but I don't think I handled it very well. I just blurted it out too fast because I was a wreck. So we weren't there fifteen minutes. He just freaked and freaked and freaked and he got in the truck and took off. He left me there all by myself! I didn't know what to do. I'd never been to a motel before so I called the police because I thought he was gonna hurt himself. I was really scared and they went, 'Ah, he'll get over it.' Later he came back and got me, but it was so freaky. The next day he came over to the apartment and we had lots of discussion about what we were gonna do. And then he told me about a place in Juarez where I could get an abortion but he didn't tell me how he knew about it.

I FOUGHT THE LAW

So we discussed our options. It was a calm discussion. There was no crying. 'I said what would make me the most happy is if you married me in Juarez and divorced me in Juarez. That way we will have been married. He didn't like that because he thought the fans would find out he was married. He was totally against that. Then he said, 'This is gonna ruin my opportunity.' Well, I wasn't gonna ruin his opportunity. There was no way that I would do something that would keep him from going forward. But I was trying to protect our parents. So I decided I would ask Bruce to marry me. He was this Air Force guy who used to show up at the bowling alley a lot. I didn't care for him at all. Randy and Robert used to work on cars and Bruce knew a lot about cars, too and that's how he wiggled his way in to our crowd. Those guys loved him. He went over to my dad's place of business, which was Northrop Aircraft, which was right next to the base, and got to know him. He took my dad out for Happy Hour every night. It was a bit of an obsession. He bought me a wedding ring and a Longines watch before I ever went out with him. And I didn't want to go out with him. I didn't really care for him. He was a user, a conniver. He was a salesman. He was thrilled. He thought he was getting a prize and I was just a girl in love with somebody else. I cried through my whole wedding. I didn't even know him. He loved that he could take me from Bobby. I told my mom that Bruce and I had got married in Juarez a few nights before and that we wanted to have a wedding in the States, and my mom and her best friend made my wedding dress. We got married in El Paso on August 1st, 1964. Bruce put me on a very short leash. All my makeup was taken away from me. I couldn't have any girlfriends over to the apartment. The night we were married I cried all night. The next day I wanted to tell him I wanted a divorce. When I was at the chapel, my dad was holding me so tight and he said, 'You don't have to do this if you don't want to,' I said, 'No daddy, I'll do it,' because I wanted to protect my mom and dad. What I didn't know was that Bruce had already told them, and they didn't need to be protected. I didn't see Bobby again. I knew he was going to California.

I first went to see Loraine when the baby was around four months old. I couldn't see her at the house because Bruce might find out, so we would meet on an odd street and park our cars and she'd come and sit with me and my baby, Allison. She was glad I kept the baby. Loraine loved me. I had Bobby's music letter sweater but it got all moth eaten. I still have the patch. Bruce threw all my pictures and memorabilia out but I have my daughter so I have the best of Bobby.

When they came back to El Paso to play the Coliseum in March, I saw him and he got to see Allison. I talked to him later that day at home and asked him what he thought of his baby. He said, 'she's all right', that she was cute, but you could tell he didn't know what to say. I sent him a long, ten page heartbreaking 'I still love you' letter after that. I said I wished we could have spent more time together. He died not long after that. I thought it was my fault. I thought after he got my letter was that it was my fault because the first reports said that he'd killed himself. I thought that my letter—and what I had said at the end, like in a wedding ceremony where it says, 'and no man shall put asunder.' That was my last line in my letter. I thought he committed suicide from my letter. I thought that for months.

The night he died, we were home by ourselves and I got about ten phone calls from, not close friends, but acquaintances that hung out at the club asking if I was alright. About the tenth call somebody told me, 'You need to go get a newspaper.' They wouldn't even tell me. I took the baby with me and I sat in the car and read it and I cried and cried. Then I went home and I called Bruce and I said, 'Can I come out to the base and talk to you?' He was drinking with all his buddies and he told me to wait. Then he said, 'I gotta go back to work. What do you want?' I showed him the newspaper and he just laughed and laughed. It was horrible. Before Bobby recorded *A New Shade Of Blue*, we sat at the piano and he sang it to me. I got so flustered. That's my favorite. And I loved *Angel Face*. Sometimes, I would think of him singing it to me. You know, for all these years I would pretend that maybe he wasn't dead, that maybe they just hid him away."

Suzie's daughter Allison remembers learning the truth when she turned eighteen. "My mom bought me a full length mirror," she relates, "and I would sit on the floor cross legged, Indian style, and stare into my mirror and look at my nose. I would just think, 'Where the hell did this come from?' 'Cause I don't look like my mom or my dad. I could never explain why I thought that but I would just stare and stare at my face in this mirror. And I would think, 'Why can I pick up any instrument right now and at least play something basic?' Because my mom and dad, the dad that I knew, couldn't carry a tune in a bucket. Then on my eighteenth birthday, I was getting dressed to go out with my boyfriend to party and I'll never forget where I was. I was in the hallway by the bathroom after finishing my makeup and she walked up to me and said, 'There's something I have to tell you.' I thought, 'whatever...' I have a keg waiting, we've got stuff to do. She said, 'I just wanted to tell you that the dad that you always knew as your dad is not your dad. Your real dad is Bobby Fuller.' I had no idea. At that point I thought to myself, 'No wonder. That makes sense', even though I didn't know who he was at all. He was just some guy. And she said, well you know that song *I Fought The Law*? And I said yeah. And

I was like, 'Oh my God, that's really weird!' And that's about it. My mom said because he was murdered not to ever look into it or say anything about it because it could be life threatening. 'Don't ever look up your uncle, don't tell anybody.' It was just too weird to think about so I put that in a place in my head and went on with my life. There have been times in my life when I needed a touch. I swear to you that song would come on the radio. I can't tell you how many times I was feeling down and I just needed a hug from my daddy. One year I found the *King Of The Wheels* album for her for Christmas and she bawled, and I freakin' bawled. I didn't really like the album. It seemed kinda goofy and I was a music snob. I always thought of Uncle Randy. I wondered where he lives. What did he look like? I wondered if he'd love me. I wonder if he would want to know that I'm here. And I would say something to her and she would say, 'No you don't! No-no-no!' But I would still say, 'I wonder what my grandma's like? I wonder if she would love me?' The stuff the little girl inside of me would think. All the things a kid would wonder."

By the time Halloween 1964 rolled around, Suzie was married and Mary was waiting out her pregnancy. Bobby retained his single status, although a ring on Pamela's finger still spoke of love and a future together. That too would crumble in the months to come.

CHAPTER TEN

---·•·---

OUR FAVORITE MARTIAN
We head for the land of fruits and nuts
and it cannot be soon enough.

"We all came out to LA together, Dewayne, me and my mother, and Bobby. And Jim Reese. Yeah we drove her Oldsmobile out the first week of November. We rented a small house at 5955 Carlton Way. An older place. I guess you could call it a kind of a cottage. We went and played for Casey Kasem out in Ventura, he was really the first DJ out there to pay attention to us, and he remained our friend and supporter. We went back to the Rendezvous and won a Battle of the Bands against horn groups, Motown groups, blues groups, other groups—we cleaned all them out and won—that's how we got the gig there."

"The first gig we got out in California got put together by Casey Kasem," said Jim. "He was DJ out there and had a big dance thing out in Thousand Oaks. We played there once a week, every week." Casey loved the band: "They were just great, always upbeat, rehearsed, fantastic. Bobby had that magnetic charm turned on all the time. Randy was a powerhouse bass player. That rhythm section was unbeatable. The Bobby Fuller Four were always one of my top groups, from the early days that they arrived in Hollywood, to the day Bobby was killed, and even after that, their sound really stood the test of time."

"I was livin' at my mom's house in Santa Ana," recalls Dewayne. "My sister and brother were there too, and then they moved to Huntington Beach and that area, Newport Beach. Bobby was shoppin' his stuff around and no one was takin' it. The Fanatics got an audition at the Rendezvous Ballroom on a Sunday. The Chantays, they were the ones that were working that particular gig at that time. We went in, it was on a Sunday, and I was like in my cowboy boots and jeans and all these other guys are dressed in these matching suits. It was just like coming into another world, really. And so they all played and we played last and the owner of the place kept us up there for two hours. And he *loved* us, man. And we played—he asked do we do this, do we do that? Bobby says, 'Well we do this and then we do this.' And then we played like our own stuff. They were *freaked* you know. And they hired us to be the house band. The Rendezvous—those were most mind blowingest shows that I've ever played, as far as people and digging it. We had a Wednesday, Thursday, Friday, and Saturday gig there. We go there on a Wednesday, Bobby Fuller and the Fanatics. And we show up and there is a line of people from out on Newport Blvd, all the way around the building to the front of the entrance. And we're drivin' up and we're all looking at each other goin', 'who are we backing up tonight?' They were there for us. And it took me twenty minutes just to get across the dance floor. We broke Dick Dale's standing room only record, and the son of the bitch wouldn't recognize it. Until the day it got burnt down, the guy that owned it told me. The Rendezvous Ballroom was where all of the old big bands used to play. Bob Keene used to play there, you know, when he was a clarinet player, or thought he was. He was a *thief*, a real good one. The Rendezvous was right on the sand, in Newport Beach. You'd walk out and there'd be ce-

I FOUGHT THE LAW

ment in the front, and you walk off that and you'd be on the sand. That would be the walk to the beach. And it was a double decker. You could go upstairs and lean over the rail, and the stage was humongous. It went close to the width of the building, except for on the left side you had a big dressing room and on the right side you had another big dressing room. And then it tiered up, you know it went up like you know how big bands used to set up where there'd be the violin section over here and this over here and that over there, and it would be on different levels, well that's how it was set up and we would play only on the first level. It held a thousand, maybe. Maybe more than that, I don't know. It was huge. And not only that, the place in the center of the room is where they did the sound. And we had to go up a ladder in the center of the room and there would be a—it almost looked like a little spaceship stuck to the ceiling, and they had windows all the way around it, you know, and there was the sound, where they ran all the sound and the light and stuff. Yeah, that was neat, man. And then it burnt down, somebody set it on fire. It was the saddest—but the guy who owned that place *loved* us. Oh man, after we auditioned, after we did all these rock and roll songs, surfer songs, you know—we even did *Miserlou*. Now Bobby could do that real good, let me tell you. Oh yeah, he could probably do it just as good as Dick Dale, far as I'm concerned. There aren't too many guitar players who could play that, I'll tell you that right now. I don't care how good they are. So we played and then when we finished, the guy asked us, 'Well, do you know this and do you know that,' and we did all the Beach Boys stuff, we did Beatles stuff, we were doin' Gerry and the Pacemakers shit. We did our own stuff, Chuck Berry, and the guy had us take over for the Chantays."

Bobby had gone back to Bob Keene at Del-Fi Records to try to interest him in the new band. Keene's studios were in disrepair and there were changes in the air there. Still, Keene was impressed by their home grown records and thought their live shows were promising.

Bob Keene explains, "They'd come to see me and I could see there were possibilities. They needed a local club to play. The Ambassador Hotel was in a section of Los Angeles that had a lot of new office buildings, similar to the middle of New York City, and I noticed that at five o'clock every day there would be thousands of young guys and gals getting out of work and heading into the street and I figured a dance band type of thing at the Hotel would go over great, and that was the first job that I myself got the guys, about a month after they came out, in December of 1964."

The Ambassador Hotel was home to the famed Cocoanut Grove nightclub for the over 21 crowd on the main floor, and downstairs was a more casual rock n' roll club for the 18-plus crowd called La Cave Pigalle. The Fanatics took it by storm, albeit under the alias of Bobby Fuller and the Cavemen.

La Cave Pigalle, or "the Pig", would showcase an early opening band starting at 5 PM for the after work crowd, and then the main act for the night would start up at 9 PM. Jeannie Romersheuser met Bobby at their first gig at the Pig right before Christmas of '64. "I lived a few blocks from the hotel and knew the people at the club, so they would let me hang around, even though I was only fifteen at the time!" laughs Jeannie. "Bobby really left an impression on me. He was the nicest person I ever met, he really was. And his shows at the club were just fantastic! I remember sometimes Dewayne would leave the drums and come out and start dancing with us in the audience and Bobby would take over on the drums and go wild!" Although Jeannie was never able to get into other clubs because of her age, she vows never to forget the shows where the band ground out sets that included dance favorites like *Land Of 1,000 Dances*, *Do You Wanna Dance*, and *I've Had It*. I remember Phil Spector sitting in at the piano with them. They were just so good, everyone loved them."

Michael Rummans of the Sloths caught the Four there as well. "I was sixteen and snuck in to see them. They played *I Fought the Law*, as well as *Miserlou*, says Michael. "I was surprised to hear that, because the British invasion was in full swing and most bands had stopped playing surf music by that time. Nevertheless, I was impressed to hear how flawlessly he played it. He was using a blonde Stratocaster. He probably had it from the surf days. After the set, I went up to ask him questions about music and bands. He was very gracious, taking time out of his break to talk with a young admirer."

Pat Montoure was sixteen when she first met Bobby, so like Jeanne and Michael, she was too young to get into the Pig. "Although we couldn't get in the club itself, we could stand by the door and see the band onstage. The thing about Bobby was he was a real flirt—as soon as he saw that you were interested in him, he would come up to you, and that's what happened that first night. He came right up to me and my friend, Pat Staudt, and we started up plans for his fan club right then, the first night we'd seen him play—from the doorway!"

"They were always a *band*," says Pat. "Even the last time I saw Bobby, which was right after they got back to L.A. after New York, he was talking about what the *band* was going to do." Pat never agreed with the story that Bobby wanted out of the band in lieu of a solo career. She explained, "All he ever wanted was to get a club like the Rendezvous—he loved that place and was real upset when it burned down. He said he wanted to play there all the time, and make records and produce records

LEFT: *The Fanatics, El Paso 1964;*
RIGHT: *Alias the Shindigs, LA 1964*

and stay put. The touring thing, with the travel and hassles and all, was what he really hated once it started up. In these early days, Bobby was happy, as all of his shows were local."

"Bobby ended up firing Jim Reese when we were playing at La Cave and Jim went home to Texas," recalls Randy. "Dewayne got his own apartment about that time. He recommended a guitar player friend. Bobby was struggling without Jim, and called him, asking him to come back to L.A. He did come back and moved in with Dewayne. He moved in with Dewayne. Mother stayed with us the whole time we were in California, both at the Carlton Way apartment and later at the Sycamore address. She took care of our clothes, and cooked for us. My dad was traveling for the gas company and was rarely home. He didn't want her to be alone at the house and neither did we."

Well, being as the Del-Fi studio was in various states of repair, the band returned to El Paso to pick up Bobby's studio equipment and take it back to Bob Keene's, to use until he had his own stuff in place. Jim: "He was in transition with the equipment, so a lot of the recording we played around with was actually on Bobby's stuff and he knew exactly how to get what he wanted out of it."

"Well we didn't sign anything with Bob Keene, you know, until later," says Dewayne. "We did our first song, *Those Memories of You*, it was like, to me it was... faggoty, I don't know. Me and Randy both felt that way. But you know, Bob Keene was always tryin' to follow the times, you know what I'm sayin'? It was kinda like away from what Bobby was, to me. But I was the new guy, you have to understand. I was a baby to them, you know, Bob, Jim Reese and all them had been together for years. And so one day, we do the song and the records come in. And they're 45s in a box, and there's probably about a hundred and fifty or whatever in a box. And we open it up, Randy and I are standing there, we open it up and says *Those Memories of You*, by BOBBY FULLER in big letters and underneath in small letters, 'and The Fanatics". And Randy went berserk, as it was agreed that the *Bobby Fuller and*—days were over. And Bob Keene says, 'Oh, this is hilarious.' And you know what—Randy goes, 'Hey BOB!' You know them big high doors, there's really two of 'em, they're real high, these doors to his office. Bob's sittin' down. He's got a picture of his gold record things in the back you know and all that shit. And Randy goes, 'What the *fuck* is this,' and throws that record like a Frisbee and luckily it went up just right in front of where it'd have cut Bob Keene's head off. It hit on the back of the wall and shattered. Randy says, 'Bobby Fuller and group, shit. Thanks a lot!' And storms out. Bob Keene was always deathly afraid of Randy. Randy, you know, he could intimidate you if he wanted to. It's been said that the fanclub thought up the name the Bobby Fuller Four. That is totally false. We were all with Bob Keene when he said, "Well what do you want it to be?" And we all said, "Well it was all four of us, wasn't it?" That's how the Bobby Fuller Four came to be. That's exactly how it came to be. Period, end of story. *Exactly* where that came from. At that time, I didn't ever keep up with the fan club crap anyway. I mean, I thought it was cool, but I was too busy wanting to learn and play and then gettin' involved in the music business."

The offending platter had been issued on Keene's Donna label (a Del-Fi subsidiary named after the Valens hit) and although DJ Jim Pewter's *Those Memories Of You* was a tepid teener, the backside was the overdriven, superphonic, fantabulous *Our Favorite Martian* which starts off with a big wash echo reverb crunch and takes off with an unbelievable surf assault, light years more wet and wild than the popular west coast bands Keene had already been working with, like the

I FOUGHT THE LAW

Lively Ones and the Sentinals.

Jim Reese claimed, "There was never a lead or rhythm guitar in the Bobby Fuller bands that I was in. Bobby and I played twin leads. I've got to say that I was totally unimpressed with surf music. I hated it back then and I hate it now. Bobby played almost all the leads on the surf instrumentals. I'd say, 'I'm sorry, I'm not into that,' and since Bobby really was, he'd do those leads. I mean, to each his own. It was seemed to me it didn't take a whole lot to play surf guitar. I mean you had to know what you were doing but there was just a certain distance you could go with it and that's it. Plus all he wanted to play was Fender guitars. Again, it was back to Buddy Holly. Bobby would give every reason in the book why we should be playing Fenders. He'd tell me that if we all played Fenders, the company would sponsor us and so I'd give him the same thing back and say if we all played Gibsons, maybe they would sponsor us."

The Donna release didn't catapult the band to the top of the charts by any means, but Keene did convince them to travel under the name the Shindigs on an immediate followup in order to get a chance to be the house band on the upcoming network teen TV music show SHINDIG as it expanded from a half hour to an hour.

Jim recalled, "I knew that some sort of negotiations were going on to get us on as the house band. YOW! Can you imagine—the Fanatics as the SHINDIG house band?"

Wolfman and *Thunder Reef* were cobbled up overnight, and spectacular and novel as both sides are, the record didn't get a pointy toed boot in the door nor did it impress anyone at ABC-TV. "Bobby wanted to make it so bad," explained Jim, "And he wanted to be accepted so much that he'd have gone with anyone who dangled something in front of him. I myself didn't know anything about Bob Keene except that he'd worked with

I FOUGHT THE LAW

Ritchie Valens and I thought that was pretty great." If Bob Keene really had told them he had created the Mustang label just for them, they surely wondered why their first big record on their very own label would be issued under an alias, and why it was number 3003. Indeed, moonlighting Arthur Lee and Johnny Echols had the first Mustang release, and they too, undercover, as the Surfettes.

Two weeks before Christmas, Sam Cooke was killed at a seedy motel after stopping in at his favorite watering hole, PJ's on Santa Monica Boulevard. Like Ritchie Valens, Sam Cooke had record business connections with Bob Keene at Del-Fi Records, which was now traveling alongside, or possibly under, the aegis of a new company called Stereo Fi Corporation. Bobby had written to Sam Coplin, a talent agent who he trusted, in Fort Worth (manager of the local garage band, the Gnats, for one) about the recent interest from Bob Keene. "I have never heard of Stereo Fi Corporation," wrote Coplin. "Are they in music publishing or what? I need a few groups to put into clubs in the Midwest and the pay is $850 a week. I have Jimmy Reed, Chuck Berry and will be booking the Ventures after January 15.'

In a 1966 print interview, Bobby described his spirits at the end of '64: "I didn't have a dime. I was living in a crummy little apartment and was miserable because I was sitting there all alone while everybody else went out Christmas shopping."

For the first time, Bobby Fuller was not in control of his recordings, or pressings, or sales, or bookings, or production, or publicity. The hazing had begun.

CHAPTER ELEVEN

LET HER DANCE
California big shots on TV and hey, the movies!
It won't be long now.

Bob Keene was in the first months of setting up the new studio and the Stereo Fi offices when the Bobby Fuller Four came in to roost. Stereo Fi headquarters, still brandishing the Del-Fi handle, was home to the new Mustang Records, as well as their in-house Maravilla Music Publishing, the Stereo Fi rack job/ cut-out operation, and soon afterward, Stars Of Tomorrow, their very own in-house talent agency that acted as the band's exclusive bookers. Keene's financial backer, Larry Nunes, was hardly a silent partner. He had learned the music trade from the bottom up, at Tip Top Music Company, located in San Francisco at 375 11th Street, a record distributorship founded by Monroe Goodman. Nunes and Goodman came as a package deal when Stereo Fi was formed, with Keene was the third wheel.

"Larry Nunes was a guy that invested in Mustang," recalls Randy. "He became partners with Bob Keene before we ever signed on. Keene had gotten a bunch of money from Nunes and we happened to come along right then, before he even had the studio running. Bobby said Nunes ran a business out of

I FOUGHT THE LAW

Bobby with Meredith McRae and Sally Field, 1965;

Long Beach that didn't seem to him to be on the up and up. One day our television went out, and Bobby said Nunes offered to give us a brand new color RCA. We drove down to Long Beach to a warehouse where Nunes ran what looked like a import/export business. He told us to pick out any thing we wanted free. Nunes came to PJ's with call girls but I don't know if you would call that a bad guy or not! I know he could get a lot of airplay on the radio stations."

The group's first Mustang label release, in December, had been the great snarling tribute to Wolfman Jack entitled *Wolfman*. The group name that appeared on the record was the Shindigs—Keene's ploy to get them on the *Shindig* TV show. Despite its excellence, that did not happen.

"*Wolfman* was not recorded by me," said Keene. "It was something that Bobby had brought with him from El Paso, or something he had worked on by himself. Same with *Our Favorite Martian*, which was better than just a surf instrumental. It was something greater."

I FOUGHT THE LAW

Randy is the voice behind the lupine growls, and it's likely that the Frantics from the Pacific Northwest were the influence with their *Werewolf*, being as Fanatics Larry Thompson and Jerry Miller were straight off the Tacoma treadmill, delivering the hard driving threat of the Northwest into the Southwest borderlands. The amazing surf instrumental *Thunder Reef*, which is really Bobby Taylor's magnificent *Thunder*—appears as the flip for this double-A fueler. It is astonishing that a single as strong as this did not land Bobby on network TV right then and there. The Mustang label got its name from the 1965 Ford Mustang, which had debuted April 17, 1964 at the New York World's Fair. The horse head label logo is virtually identical to the Ford profile icon. Whether Keene's Bronco affiliate was also a nod to the Ford firm of the same moniker remains a fact unconfirmed.

Hair by Jay Sebring

"I was still finishing up my studio when they came into town," said Keene. "They put up some of the interior walls, they put up cork in the walls in the booths, and they worked with the echo chambers all over. Because our studio wasn't ready, they did some recording down in Arizona in order to get a new record done."

The group traveled out to Audio Recorders in Phoenix, Arizona to record for two weeks. Bob Keene said that Bobby insisted on recording there, even though local L.A. studios were certainly available. Audio Recorders was where Lee Hazlewood was pumping out Duane Eddy's chart topping instrumentals, and Bobby was eager to learn more about their technique. Two songs that were cut at Audio Recorders, *Take My Word* and *She's My Girl* would make it to wax as the first Bobby Fuller Four Mustang single, while *Pamela* remained unissued for years. This outstanding tribute to his fiancée back in Texas is truly to Fuller what *Peggy Sue* is to Buddy Holly.

Take My Word/She's My Girl was delivered to local radio stations and started to make noise in the charts. This motivated Keene and company into getting the group a decent place to showcase. That place would be PJ's, the same place that Trini Lopez made it, and where the Standells had gotten their Hollywood start. Both Trini and the Standells, and many other primarily jazz artists, would record live albums at the club after getting popular there.

The Bobby Fuller Four opened at PJ's on March 15. Bobby received telegrams from Phil Spector and Ahmet Ertegun congratulating him on his making an early mark on the Hollywood scene.

"PJ's was awesome," recalls Dewayne. "All these people used to come in there, it was like *big time*. When you first walked into the place, that was the jazz lounge. Yeah, it was all jazz and it was so cool. And then you walk through into the back, and then you'd walk through a little area and it would be like this black guy who was in the men's room, and it was I guess where you kinda hung your coat and everything, and then you walked on in and this guy named Larry would greet you and you would come in the door and in the kitchen—the food was awesome—it was the neatest place, really. I mean, the atmosphere at that time was so awesome, they called it the City of Glitter, it was actually in the air. Glitter. Or maybe that's my imagination. The guy that owned PJ's opened It's Boss. He took us from there and put us over there. We were real hot at that time. You know, I mean, we even backed up Chuck

I FOUGHT THE LAW

Berry. Yeah, and then the cool thing about that was Bobby loved Chuck Berry. And we knew all the Chuck Berry songs. We went to this place, it was out by the airport, I can't remember the name of it, but these guys used to come in PJ's and wanted us to play out there. So finally Bob Keene hooked up some kind of a figure and we got to play there. And uh, it was a real cool place—it's now a porn place, you know what I mean? But then one night we showed up to play and we didn't even know we were backing up Chuck Berry. He walked in and he's an arrogant asshole and he goes, "I hope you guys are better than the band that was in here last night." Well he starts off and didn't realize that he was dealing with some boys that knew his material and he was in heaven the rest of the evening. He forgot we were white. We were hooked up because of that, because we were right there, Carlton Way was just down the street from Del-Fi, like, maybe, six walking blocks. And we would get up every morning, and be at Del-Fi Records at nine o' clock and start recording. Doin' whatever we were gonna do, before we ever did anything. I mean, we were like, no one even knew we

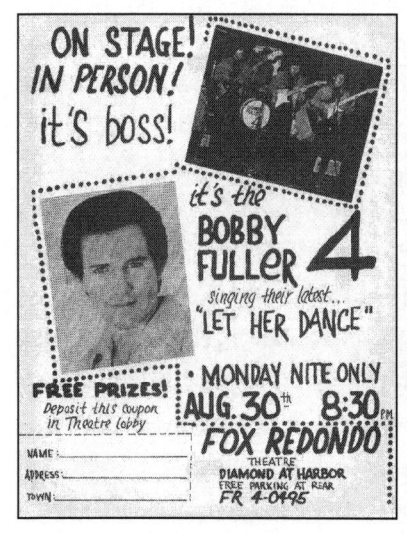

I FOUGHT THE LAW

existed, let's put it that way."

"It seems like we were always at PJ's," said Jim Reese. "We were booked for four to six week stretches, so it really became a second home for us." When Paul Raffles, the owner, decided to open a teen club (over 25 not admitted) on Sunset Strip, he chose Bobby's band over nine big contenders which included the Turtles to open the club, which was called It's Boss. Between the new club and PJ's, the Four had constant work.

The first record with hit potential for the band was coming up. Back home in El Paso, Bobby had recorded his composition, *Keep On Dancing*, an infectious, Valens-ish romper, but it was a few light years behind what it grew up to be—the blazing *Let Her Dance* was a statement of the Bobby Fuller Four sound, entirely unreliant on the British beat, explosive and pounding. The June release of the record had it in the charts immediately, and it took off coast to coast. The booming drums, the great Tex-Mex surge of the guitars—even that typewriter bell sound that totally makes the record.

LEFT: *Ad for Celebrity Night at PJ's 1965;*
RIGHT: *The Bobby Fuller Four: Dewayne Quirico, Randy Fuller, Jim Reese, Bobby Fuller, 1965 Aldo*

Bob Keene compared *Let Her Dance* to some of his own earlier productions: "Remember *Hippy Hippy Shake*? Well, that was also the Valens band that I used on that. And there was another song called *Cherrystone* by the Addrisi Brothers and that sound was very successful. And we tried to use that to a degree with the same feeling in *Let Her Dance*, and that's where that all came from. It was new, it was a brand new sound and that's why I was interested in it. The Coke bottle—I was looking for a percussion sound and one of the guys was drinking Coke. So I remember we filled it with water and we kept changing the water level to get the right tone. We were looking to develop new sounds. Liberty, of course, came up with the Chipmunks which was where they had spit up the tape. And they had another one called *The Big Hurt* or something where they had two sheets in sync and then they would go out of sync, which would give it a phasing affect, and things like that. We all had to kind of use what we had on hand to try to develop something new, because we didn't have all the electronic stuff that they have today. I think Bobby was admiring of the Beach Boys. Yeah, he really dug their stuff. I mean he didn't want everybody to sound like Buddy Holly, it's just that that's where he was. But you've gotta remember that he hadn't been around a hell of a lot, he hadn't been out of Texas much or El Paso, and so he really hadn't been exposed to a lot of different things like he would be if he was in New York or Philadelphia or something like that. Out here in Los Angeles, you just didn't get that cross-section of musical talent and musical expression that you got on the east coast. There wasn't very much similarity between the east coast music and the west coast music."

Howard Steele talks about Del-Fi Studios. "You know, I don't know who designed it, but the acoustic sounds of it were as good as you could expect for a small room. You know, it wasn't much wider than, while I'm standing here, from the back of this car to here. And one wall was wood but it was really fine zigzag, saw tooth, and the ceiling was padded over, the walls were padded, it was the kind of studio that was hard to play in because you couldn't *hear* anything, and you'd put the headphones on but it would still be muffled. There was a bank below. And when the bank's air conditioning was on, it would shake everything in the studio. So when we did vocals and stuff, this engineer, unknown to the band, had wired a switch to turn off the air conditioning. It was on the wall, we'd flip the air conditioning off, do the vocals, turn it back on. But *very* advanced electronics. A guy named John Stevens built the consul and it was one of the first eight-track machines. It sounded good in there! I mean, the control room sounded good. The building was right on the corner of Selma and Vine Streets. It got repossessed when they chained up the doors at Del-Fi."

"When *Let her Dance* came out in July on Liberty, we were really surprised," says Randy. "Bobby, who understood the music business better than the rest of us, said there was something going on. In LA, *Let Her Dance* was on the radio for weeks. That takes a lot of dough or connections. One time, Larry took some of our pictures, wearing those red suits from the *I Fought The Law* album cover, and he had these life size cardboard figures made of each of us and then he got Wallichs Music City in Hollywood to place them in the main entrance. At the time, Wallichs was the top music store in Hollywood. We went down and signed autographs. In that respect Larry Nunes was a real go-getter. He sure made us feel like a million dollars."

"Larry Nunes who was close to the guys at Liberty, and they wanted to put out a record on Bobby Fuller," said Keene. "That was *Let Her Dance*. They claimed that they had the rights to release it, that we'd made a deal with them, which we hadn't.

I FOUGHT THE LAW

LEFT: *Phil Spector with Randy and Bobby at La Cave Pigalle, 1965;* RIGHT: *Bobby Fuller, booted and buckled*

But I mean, Liberty was kind of a record label that was into all kinds of bullshit deals. I mean, they were always getting into lawsuits and stuff. Al Bennett was kind of a bad boy. We were playing golf when the thing came up and we just, you know, in the conversation—the next thing I know, the guy claims that he has rights. That took about a month to get resolved and then that's when we came out with it. Of course, we lost the impact on *Let Her Dance* because we were on to *I Fought The Law*."

Dewayne continues, "I remember one day we played this gig and this was the first time we ever heard ourselves on the air. That was the most exciting night of my life. Well we played this little concert like in Santa Ana—hell, it was almost like a high school kind of thing. It was Cannibal and the Headhunters and the Stage Coachmen. I was throwin' my sticks in the audience at the end of it, and we all felt cool and then we get in the Greenbriar, we're all in it and we're drivin' and we're just getting on the freeway and on the radio comes on—*Let Her Dance*. And we all just—well there's just no feeling like it. I mean, I don't care how much money you got, you'll never be able to buy anything like that. It was probably KRLA, or probably KFWB. No, it was probably KFWB, the big powerhouse. It was Casey Kasem. He loved everything in the world. You know, the funny thing is when we started working with Casey, we went out to Dallas and he had a teen thing out there, and Bob Keene got us a gig with him and he took us sight unseen, and Casey Kasem's never done that. And then when we played, the girls were all comin' up to the band, it was unbelievable. It was really—I mean, they'd never heard of us. And there they are, man, and we're kickin' ass and Bob Keene walks in, he's like—he couldn't believe it, you know, and all he saw was dollar signs ringin' around in there."

Paul Politi had come to Mustang and a young promotion man when *Let Her Dance* was released. He recalls, "I first heard of Bobby when Keene played me a couple of songs that he was working on with him. I believe the first thing I heard was a kind of a surfing song, written by Jim Pewter. Yeah, it was a demo. I liked Bobby, and he told me it was a group from El Paso and he was a big Ritchie Valens fan. I had first met Bob Keene in 1961. I had a record that I wrote and produced called *Those Oldies But Goodies* by Little Caesar and the Romans. I was just outta high school, Belmont High. I think I was sixteen. From time to

LEFT: *Bobby with Roger Christian;*
RIGHT: *The Four with confusing signage*

time, I would bring in songs that I had written and produced. Anyway, the next time I heard about Bobby was when I was hired to do promotion for Mustang Records. That was when *Let Her Dance*, was out and was a hit in Los Angeles and I believe Pittsburgh also. Liberty had put the record out. The record was kind of a local hit and Larry Nunes, who was Bob Keene's partner, made a deal with Al Bennett of Liberty Records and they put it out, and I think they lost the record. You know, I think it was a hit in a couple of markets and then they wanted to spread it. And they gave it to Liberty and Liberty just kind of lost it. It was a *great* record, I thought. One of my favorite songs was the flip side, *Another Sad And Lonely Night*. It's really underrated. It's one of the best things that Bobby did. So anyway, I started working for Mustang doing national promotion and *I Fought The Law* was coming out. Bob called me and hired me to do extra promotion. I had promoted my own song, *Those Oldies But Goodies*, 'cause it was my record, not even knowing what I was doing. But I think I impressed Bob and so he hired me. I remember Larry Nunes gave me the record. I didn't know Larry but he was huge in the record distribution business. And he had something like twelve or thirteen offices in eleven western states. What a lot of people don't realize—there were certain markets like Bakersfield—every record that was sold there went through Larry Nunes, he was Record Service and he was Tip Top Music. Bob Keene was in financial problems and Larry Nunes was the one who put the money up. He was probably in his fifties. He, at one time, was a Golden Gloves boxer, kind of a street guy, Portuguese. He started up in San Francisco with an older guy by the name of Monroe Goodman. And Larry kinda came in and built that company into, like I said—they had twelve or thirteen offices. They were in Dallas, they were in Denver, they were in Seattle, Spokane,

I FOUGHT THE LAW

Portland, San Diego, Los Angeles, Las Vegas. They were a rack job mainly. They had no connections in New York, just in eleven western states. Larry Nunes had a big distribution set up, so one of the first things I did was started doing was working with the offices in the eleven western states. The office in Los Angeles had about a hundred employees. They had girls that worked in the office, and one of the things that they would do, the first thing in the morning, there was KFWB. Larry had *all* of the girls calling in and requesting *I Fought The Law*. They used to have battles of the records, the new records, and that's why *I Fought The Law* always did really well. I went down there, Bob brought me down, to meet Larry and he took me around and said, 'Pick out some forty-fives.' And I think this surprised Bobby, and Bob Keene too. He said, "Any record that's hot, any record that this guy wants, anything—give him whatever he wants." In other words, he wanted to know what was going on in order to compare records. So if Bobby or Bob Keene wanted or wanted to hear something, anything that was new and exciting, he wanted us to have whatever we needed. And so he told everyone at their company that they almost kind of *worked* for me. Del-Fi had just a studio and a small office on Selma, it was over a medium-sized bank. Bob Keene had some stationary that said, 'Assets over 20 million dollars,' because we were right over the vault. It being used as an echo chamber was just mythology. I think they used a hall and then they had, later on, an actual echo chamber. The hallway was one of those where you'd say a word and you could just hear yourself. It was just natural, it wasn't built that way, it just happened. That was Bob Keene's original echo chamber when I did *Those Oldies But Goodies*. And then later on, Larry Nunes gave him money to build one. They redid the whole studio. Larry Nunes put in good money, because before that they really didn't have the money to do the studio. But with Larry's money, they had some really talented guys in there that built it, state-of-the-art. If I'm not mistaken, I think four-track was the big thing, maybe eight-track. We were one of the only studios in town that had that. Larry put some real good money into the company. The interesting thing about it that Keene told me, and this tells you about Bobby Fuller—I *really* liked Bobby Fuller, he was unbelievable. He played everything. He *really*, really loved music. But he was more than just an artist, he could have been a huge A&R man. He had a great ear, great ideas. And he had a great

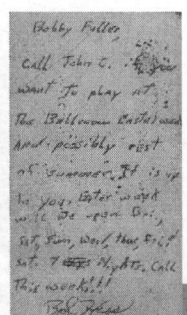

LEFT: *Dewayne and Randy, 1965;*
RIGHT: *Original Rendezvous Ballroom card/ business proposition*

heart. Keene told me exactly—when Bobby went out and Keene was trying to build the studio—when he came back, he had a studio in El Paso and brought a lot of his equipment and made it available to Bob Keene. That's the kind of guy he was. I'll never forget that. By that time, the money was being put in so Keene had some high-priced guys putting in that kind of stuff. They had a guy by the name of Roger Stanwich that worked on the staff. He was a genius in his own right who had some unbelievable ideas, so Keene used him, and he was also the guy that kept everything working. One day he came into the office and he had a photograph that was not exactly Cape Canaveral, but of a rocket launch out in the desert. And it was a rocket that he launched! I mean, it wasn't a firecracker or nothing; it was a big thing. It was very impressive, at least at that period of time, 'cause that kind of showed the type of guy he was. There are all kinds of rumors that go around, but this is the truth. The air conditioning for the bank was right over our recording studio. In other words, we were over the vault. I want to say that we were over the vault, but that could have been Keene 'cause he put that around. But anyway, the air conditioning for the bank was right over our studio. And when you were recording, you could hear the vibration of the air conditioning—the hum. So Robert went up in the attic and he set up a thing and we had a switch, so whenever we did vocals in the recording studio, we would switch off the air conditioning for like, six minutes. Then when we were done, we would turn it back on. One day, I don't know what happened but we forgot to turn it back on and the air conditioning guys were there, and they were going crazy to find out why there was no air conditioning! And then, "Oh!" we remembered it and turned it back on, and so the guys never found the switch. He was an electronics wizard. Bobby was working at PJ's when I got there.

I FOUGHT THE LAW

LEFT: *Telegrams from Phil Spector and Ahmet Ertegun at PJ's opening, March 1965*

Larry Nunes was the one who got him the gig. When I used to go out to Larry Nunes' place, 'cause Larry sold so many records, the head guys at Capitol and RCA, or the sales managers, they would be sitting in the lobby, waiting for him. He would have to sign the checks, and I mean big checks. And I used to be able to go right into his office, and Larry would be sitting in there with his friend playing poker. And all the guys are sitting out there, the heads of distributors and labels. It's different now, the companies don't mean as much as they used to. But back in the old days, there was Capitol, there was Columbia, there was Decca, and then there were the independents. And in each market, especially in Los Angeles, there might've been five or six independent distributors. So it was great for the independents, because first of all, the independents had a good piece of the action. Rock and roll and rhythm and blues—Columbia didn't even *cut* any rock and roll. They were like the last ones to come into rhythm and blues. You know, they were kinda still doing Doris Day and Rosemary Clooney and that kinda stuff. That's when I first got into business, the distributor was a very important thing. For instance, you had a label, you could appreciate it because you were an independent. With distribution today, you either go with the independents who really don't have very much power or do very much, or you go with a major. If you make the wrong choice, like Keene or Larry Nunes did with Liberty, you're kind of dead, 'cause you're tying yourself up with a distribution deal for two or three years, whatever it is. But back then, the exciting thing about the record business was the independents. You know, that's why the business kind of fell apart once the independents—the *real* independents disappeared. Say your record's happening or your group's happening or your artist is happening. Let's say Los Angeles is not *happening*. Well, you take your records out of the distributorship and go right across the street to another distributorship and give 'em the record that you didn't sell. See, you change the whole thing. You *tweak* it. So if Cleveland wasn't happening, you go across the street to the other guy. So they had to kind of take care of you. It was an easy thing, it wasn't a big thing, you could do it right in the middle of the record! And then *boom!* All of the sudden, your record is getting played in Cleveland. It was more of an exciting thing. The independent guy had more power, you see.

"I remember the last tour before Bobby died. Bobby was a writer. He wasn't in the music business for just glory, he cared about music and that was his first love. He wasn't going crazy over the girls and he wasn't going around showing off. He was just a very solid guy that really cared about what he was doing with a lot of beliefs and a lot of goals. I mean, he played every instrument. I think he taught Dewayne how to play the drums. And one of the things that I remember about Bobby, and Barry was there that day, Barry White. Bobby was really upset having to go on the road for Bob Keene. He felt that he could write songs better than the caliber he was being offered, but Keene was trying to get him to go to some of these hot guys, hot songs. Bobby was kinda disappointed with the quality of the songs that they were being offered. And Bobby didn't really want to be going around touring. Maybe just staying at PJ's would have been okay. Keene wanted him on the road, promoting and touring, and Bobby's first thought wasn't being on the road, his first thought was coming out with the best record. There was a conflict there. Bobby was very upset. He wasn't whiney, he wasn't belligerent, but he wasn't happy. Everything was kind of worked through Bob Keene, to a degree, but Bobby had carte blanche. I remember a particular receptionist, and this tells you a lot about Bobby Fuller. It was something they did in the studio, it could have been *I'm A Lucky Guy*. But Bobby went and did something in the studio and it was *unbelievable*. I remember Barry was there and *he* was impressed with Bobby Fuller. It was one of those once-in-a-lifetime kind of things. And we're all in a high, everybody was excited, Randy and Jimmy and I'm not sure if it was Dalton or Dewayne. I think it was Dalton. Everybody's going, 'Play it back! Oh that sounds great! This is gonna be big!' It was just the kind of thing going on for maybe twenty minutes, hearing it over and over. And then Bobby says, 'We can't do it. We're gonna have to take it off.' It was a thing that was real important in the song and he took it off. And Bob say, 'What? Are you crazy?' But Bobby said, 'We can't have it,' because Bobby's whole thing was that whatever they did on a record, they had to be able to duplicate without effects. In other words, with the four guys in person. I think it was an overdub or something. And I'm telling you, and this is the Lord's truth, you'll never appreciate *Let Her Dance* until you've heard it in person. It's even better than the record. Bobby wasn't a gimmick guy. He was a guy that believed, 'When we play our music, the audience isn't gonna be disappointed, we're gonna play it *better* than the record.' And like I said, that's why he would've made a great A&R man. That was his whole concept for the Bobby Fuller Four. I remember he would be listening to other artists and what they did, and that was part of his thing, he wouldn't go to the gimmick. I remember he was kind of impressed with Neil Diamond, because at that time *Cherry Cherry* had come out. But Bobby was straight-ahead rock and roll, very talented guy. Bobby didn't like New York. I remember they did a club called Ondine's, and that was kind of tied in with when Keene went. I think what happened was they did Ondine's and then Keene met up with them and they went around to some of the New York publishers. And that's when they found *Magic Touch*, which was a Copperman-Rubens song. *I'm A Lucky Guy* was Bob Crewe, who had the Four Seasons. Keene was always in a hurry. He wanted to do things the fast way. So that was his idea, let's go get a bunch of great songs. That might've been good for some groups, but not for Bobby Fuller. I'm not saying he didn't like

Celebrity Night At PJ's

I FOUGHT THE LAW

The Bobby Fuller Four, 1965
Dewayne, Bobby, Jim and Randy

The Magic Touch, but based on what he heard, I think he was disappointed. Keene would tout, 'You're gonna get all these great songs, and it's gonna make it easier on you.' Keene spent a lot of time in the mastering process, which is a whole different thing. A lot of guys, they go in the studio and it's all done in the studio. Whatever's done in the mastering depends on the record company. But Keene spent a lot of time with that. But with Bobby, the harmonics and the overtones in *Let Her Dance*, oh man! You can understand why Phil Spector *really* liked Bobby Fuller. That song... you had to hear it in person, I heard it at maybe twenty different venues and different types of venues. And I didn't care who was around, when *Let Her Dance* came on, it just kept building and building, it was like a train! If I'm not mistaken, Larry Nunes *sued* Liberty Records because they *didn't do* anything. It's like how a lot of records will start and a label buys them. Well in this case, they didn't do anything. I wasn't there at the time, but they must have had other records that were happening or more important or whatever, and I think they were doing it more because Larry Nunes was doing them a favor. Liberty Records, at that time, didn't have their own distributors. I guess they worked with independents, I don't know. I don't care what label you're in, you can't go into a radio station with five records and say, 'Play 'em all.' You go in with one record. A lot of it has to do with your priorities. And, you know, timing is *very* important. *Let Her Dance* was lost. *Let Her Dance*, in my opinion, could've been a bigger record than *I Fought The Law*. The thing is, *I Fought The Law* got a better push."

Liberty's full page ad for *Let Her Dance* in *Billboard* was a waste of time, as the brakes were about to be put on it by Mustang. The July 17 issue of *Billboard* noted that, "The Bobby Fuller Four appeared in area department stores promoting their Mustang single *Let Her Dance*. Label now negotiating with a major company to handle national release for the disk." The

The Bobby Fuller Four, PJ's 1965

following week, the music trade magazine reported, "Hollywood—Liberty Records will handle the national and international distribution of the Bobby Fuller Single *Let Her Dance* on the Mustang label. Robert Keene, president of Stereo-Fi made the announcement. Fuller and band are playing at PJ's."

Let Her Dance was re-released by Mustang with a new catalog number when Liberty withdrew distribution. Having lost its momentum, it crested and rested at a disappointing #26 position on the *Billboard* charts.

CHAPTER TWELVE

HOLLYWOOD A GO-GO
Guys from Chicago make the scene
and hairdressers come to PJ's.

The origins of PJ's, the Los Angeles night club that had become home to the Bobby Fuller Four, were not on the west coast at all, but on the northside of Chicago. Paul Raffles, Pat Fontecchio, and Bill Doherty had bought out the Black Orchid there in 1956 from night club pioneer Al Greenfield, who had opened the club in 1949. Located at 101 East Ontario, the show bar, which became a favorite hangout for Hugh Hefner who learned a lot from the club before developing his own Playboy Club, featured singers and comedians like Larry Storch and Shecky Green; and singers like Tony Bennett and Johnny Mathis got their start at the Black Orchid. Mathis broke all attendance records at the club in 1957, and that Christmas was presented with a diamond crusted gold watch from the owners. When the Orchid was faced with tax challenges a year and change later, Raffles and Doherty declared bankruptcy and headed west at the end of 1959. Plans were already in place for them to develop a jazz club in Hollywood along the same lines as the Orchid, with major financing from millionaire shoeman Harry Karl, whose biographical details will reveal themselves

I FOUGHT THE LAW

LEFT: *The Bobby Fuller Four, 1966* - Randy, Bobby, Dalton Powell and Jim Reese; RIGHT: Bobby, 1966

shortly. Chuck Murano and Elmer Valentine, an old friend and ex-cop from Chicago, respectively, came in as partners. Two years into PJ's, Valentine would sell his way out of PJ's to open the Whisky A Go-Go.

PJ's opened it's doors at 8151 Santa Monica Boulevard in February of 1961. It featured a cozy layout with front and back rooms which were made to contain separate entertainment on any given night. With a brazen no cover, no minimum policy and an offbeat Hollywood persona, it enjoyed immediate popularity. By the time the Bobby Fuller Four had come in with a residency, PJ's was a destination jazz club, with top rank entertainment. Several live albums had been recorded at PJ's, including Eddie Cano, Rufus Thomas, Trini Lopez, and the Sin-Say-Shuns. Just before the BF4, the Standells had recorded and released their first album *The Standells In Person At PJ's*.

Joyce Quirico remembers the early days at PJ's as a teenage regular. "I dated Paul Raffles briefly but if I had known he was married and the right answer to the question, "Do you know what a golden shower is?" I might have thought again! I found out the hard way and said, 'whoa, let me out of here!'

The owners at that time were Chuck Moriarty, Paul Raffles,

I FOUGHT THE LAW

Al Loeb, Bill Doherty, and Elmer Valentine. They were all small investors, and they would hang out at this big round table by the kitchen window—they served breakfast after hours. It was right by the dance floor. So they all would sit at that table. I had a girlfriend who was going out with Al Loeb. I don't want to say they were Mafia. I would say they were heavy crime—drugs, prostitution, they weren't killers. I never knew of Eddie Nash. I heard he owned Losers, but not PJ's. I worked at Gazzari's for like, fifteen minutes. I was everywhere. I was a wild child. I knew everybody's business. My cousin was Red Buttons and he got me into the Screen Actors Guild. That's where I met Dale. She was dating Randy. I was dating Dewayne. This woman, Melody, was in PJ's almost every night with Bobby. Nothing special to look at. I never got the feeling that Bobby liked her, you know, that way. She was working for Larry Nunes and Bob Keene just to keep girls away from Bobby and keep him happy. It was her job. Randy once said that he didn't think Bobby ever really found the right girl, that he was just into the music. He was kind of shy, like of awkward, really. He wasn't sophisticated. He was a Texas boy, polite. I was used to a faster crowd. Bobby wasn't real forward. He has a sort of sweetness about him, a determination about him. He never really seemed to be into conversation. When I got together with Dewayne, we would hang out with Randy, but Bobby never hung out with us. I was there the night they recorded *I Fought The Law*. I was there all night. It was a long night! And I can guarantee you that any rumors about anybody else playing the drums on that song are wrong. I was there the whole night. Dewayne played the drums on *I Fought The Law*. Period."

Bob Keene was good at picking up on people immediately. I didn't like him. In fact, I hated him the minute I met him. He shook my hand, and I wanted to peel my skin off and soak it in acid. Nothing that came out of his mouth was the truth. I didn't meet Rick Stone until after Bobby died. He was never there, never at the shows, never at PJ's. I have a good memory and was very observant and he wasn't there! Before I met the band, I was doing go-go dancing at a place called the Pussycat A Go-Go and *Let Her Dance* and *Another Sad and Lonely Night* were on the jukebox and I played and danced to them all the time.

Rock and roll television was busting loose in 1965. The BF4 appeared on *Shebang* and *Shivaree* in late June, the band went on to appear on *The Lloyd Thaxton Show*, too. *Hollywood A Go-Go* was next. Spun from a local rock and roll dance blast called *Ninth Street West* on Channel 9 KHJ-TV, the hour long show quickly became the yardstick for teen talent programming. Donalie Young was the producer of *Hollywood A Go-Go*, and "playola" was apparently in its business plan. She recalls the trade off that got the Bobby Fuller Four onto the show on November 6, 1965. Her husband Barry Young was, at the time, clicking with a mundane pop number on Columbia called *One Has My Name*. Barry's push was coming from Philadelphia star maker Bob Marcucci, who can be either blamed or lauded for the creation and proliferation of teen heart throbs Fabian and Frankie Avalon. Chancellor Records founder Marcucci had relocated to the west coast to further work his wiles and had begun building the career of Barry Young.

"*One Has My Name* was recorded before Marcucci came into our lives and was admittedly helped along by the manager of the Bobby Fuller Four, who was a record wholesaler," recalls Ms. Young in her memoir. "Of course, I would put the Bobby Fuller Four on my television show—if he would order 10,000 copies of Barry's record!" There is little doubt as to who this manager/wholesaler was, and this type of deal was typical, rather than exceptional, in the popular music scene of the day. Barry Young would be dead a month later from a brain abscess. The ten thousand record deal likely ended up as a cutout, as Tip Top was running cutouts for them. Tip Top got the Bobby Fuller Four television exposure that they had bargained for, and ran the resales for the doomed Columbia single. This is known in the business as a "win-win" situation.

The trade offs continued. A radio jingle for Gallenkamp Shoes to the tune of *Let Her Dance* was also cut as a favor trade. The popular Gallenkamp shoe brand was nationally distributed by Karl's Shoes, the largest privately held shoe store chain in the US at the time. The company was owned by PJ's boss Paul Raffles' father-in-law, multi-millionaire Harry Karl, who is described in FBI records as "an associate of many hoodlums arriving in Los Angeles from Chicago". Karl's ties with Chicago and Hollywood "Mickey Mouse" mobsters are legion, and his mob-associated friends included everyone in the music and motion picture industry from Columbia Pictures boss Harry Cohn to Frank Sinatra. Syndicated newspaper columnist

LEFT: *Bobby promo shot*; RIGHT: *Bobby, Jim Reese, Randy with the Greenbrier van, 1966*

I FOUGHT THE LAW

LEFT: *Bobby at Album Avenue, 1964;*
RIGHT: *Randy and Bobby, 1965*

Dorothy Kilgallen reported the 1958 marriage of Judith Karl and Paul Raffles at the same time that she slipped in a scoop about Harry Karl being set to marry Harry Cohn's widow Joan, an arrangement put together by Sidney Korshak. Judith Karl Raffles drew socialites and stars into PJ's via her father's deep connections with Hollywood stars and their accountants, so to speak. Chicago Outfit strategist John "Handsome Johnny" Roselli, who was sponsored into the Friars Club of Beverly Hills by Frank Sinatra in 1963, was named in FBI files as a contact for Karl. A friend of Jack Rubenstein, a/k/a Jack Ruby, from their mutual Chicago night club days, Roselli was involved in the CIA plot to assassinate Fidel Castro, and is believed to have been part of the assassination plot of John F. Kennedy, just weeks after he, Roselli, had acquired Friars Club membership status. That Jack Ruby was unknown to the Black Orchid people during their respective Chicago night club days is unlikely. That said, PJ's roots were indeed in Chicago and deeply associated with the Chicago mob, a/k/a the Outfit, which found Hollywood's glitter and gold quite interesting.

The association between Paul Raffles, Judie (Judith) Karl and Donalie Young of *Hollywood A Go-Go* had begun back in

I FOUGHT THE LAW

Chicago, where Donalie met Paul at his Black Orchid nightclub. Romance initially blossomed for the pair, but it faded quickly, as Paul was on to the greener pastures of his future wife Judith Karl and her millionaire, showbiz loving father. Donalie would recall being snubbed by Paul after they had both, separately, relocated to Los Angeles, she as a single mother and he with Judy and their new baby. No matter how many shoes were sold, or records traded, each maneuver served to push the Bobby Fuller Four deeper into teenage ears.

By mid-65 the British Invasion was in full swing. In six months, the band had moved ahead at warp speed, and although their promotion was entirely out of their hands, they played all of the shows and engagements and took on all of the fan meet and greets like the stars they had always been. Times were changing, but for those few months in mid-1965, teenagers still held sway in the charts and there was still a carefree mood on the radio. That was about to change. The Watts riots would take out a huge section of Los Angeles, and a general malaise was about to take on the surf and turf crowd. Greas-

LEFT: *Bobby Fuller style*; RIGHT: *Bobby with Arlene Coletti at the Phone Booth, NYC 1966*

I FOUGHT THE LAW

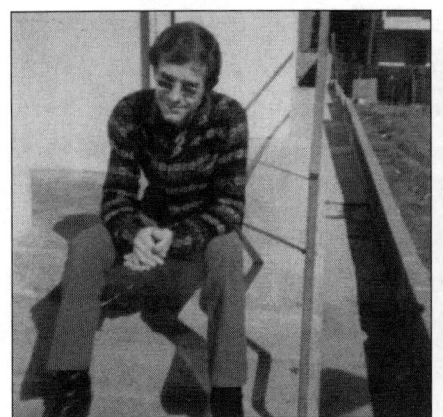

Boss threads, pretty girls 1966

ers and hodads were about to be phased out. Randy was starting to grumble loudly about wanting long hair like his friends in the Standells, who'd gone from wearing their hair slicked back to combing it forward like the Beatles. Randy appealed for help. "Maybe if everybody lets our manager know they like long hair..." pleaded Randy in a local teen paper.

Randy's pleas fell on deaf ears with Jay Sebring, the hair stylist to all of the truly happening stars, including the Four. At the time Jay was dating El Paso beauty Sharon Tate, Suzie's old classmate. Sebring would fall victim to the Manson family in August of 1969, along with his moneyed partner, coffee heiress Abigail Folger, and lady Sharon. Bobby on the other hand, wasn't concerned about keeping up with foreign bands when it came to looks. When quizzed, Bobby described their *look* as a "mixture of the Continental style and Western". Usually dressed in streamlined slacks and jackets, their stage clothes included thin ties and pointy boots, and their hair was what one can describe as longish pompadours done in a well-groomed style, with good sideburns and no facial hair. The pointy boots were not from Karl's, but from an exclusive shop on Hollywood Boulevard and set the guys back $125 a pair, big money in 1965.

I FOUGHT THE LAW

"They were a combination of cowboy boots and Cuban-heeled roach stompers," recalls Randy, "like Beatle boots only cooler and wilder, and cut real, real high—almost to the knee."

August featured some big, big shows, including the huge KFWB afternoon blast at the Rose Bowl with Herman's Hermits, the Guilloteens, Thee Midniters, and the Turtles—admission, one dollar!

Rick Stone called the show 'a real trophy on Bob's dashboard'. "The Bobby Fuller Four stole that show completely," he recalled. "It was wild! Kids were going totally crazy for them!" Jim Reese recalls that the band was forced to use all Vox equipment at this major show, and they were furious. Immediately after the Rose Bowl show both bands raced to San Diego for another blast with the Hermits but this time they refused to play without trusty Fender amps. 'The Hermits came over to us and begged that we let them use our equipment. They said they couldn't stand Vox shit either and they were nuts for our good ol' Fender amps!" said Jim Reese. "They were real grateful when we let 'em use them!"

Randy recalls the Rose Bowl show differently. To his abject horror, someone had ordered up stage wear for the band that he found totally objectionable. The odd suits were delivered

LEFT: *Jim Reese and Jimmy Gilmer flank the fake Sir Doug, 1966*; RIGHT: *Bobby, star pic*

just in time.

"I was told that Nudies was making us these Western suits," recalls Randy, "and I get home and I've got this this *clown* outfit waiting for me. I could not get into it. And I'm going, 'Man, this is not *me*.' Well, Dewayne says, 'Oh, you've got a nice ass, girls'll like it.' I'd been hiding the whole time with that stupid red suit on. I tore the pants the day that we were gonna wear them. So we started arguing about it and fighting and *bam* the whole butt rips out of my pants. My mother just sewed it back up and I put 'em back on and... here we go. And we lucked out sitting on a red convertible. I sat on top of it like we had just come out on the football field. I think they just bought the cars out for that Rose Bowl thing. You know, and everybody else, they weren't going that route. I must have been ahead of my time, or I did too many drugs or something. I mean, you got four guys dressed up in clown suits. They were made at Nudies, yeah, and they were supposed to be Western outfits. They looked more like space outfits from—I don't know, like what a space rocket rider would wear. Or like something the Temptations would wear. Who in the hell designed these things? And why—why me?"

LEFT: *Bobby behind 1776 Sycamore, 1966;*
RIGHT: *Bobby rests in the van, 1966*

I FOUGHT THE LAW

Randy's wife Dale recalls his shame, "It was a really big show and he felt so humiliated. Randy came into the audience to tell me how much he hated them. He was really mad!"

While Randy was brooding about the double-knit mod suits, the stunning *Never To Be Forgotten* slipped out to the stations and stores in September with the reissued *Let Her Dance*—quite the twin spin, but it missed its true moment in the limelight when, three weeks later, *I Fought The Law* hit the racks. The song had been their calling card since their Fanatics days, when Randy first pulled the 1960 album track off his *In Style With The Crickets* album back in El Paso. It had sold well as a their own Texas recording on Exeter and had always been a staple in their sets. Bobby had even sat in on the song with the Crickets, back at the Golden Key Club. It crashed the gates of every radio station that Stereo-Fi serviced—with enticements, says Keene, "The only reason we got *I Fought The Law* on KHJ, which was the number one radio station out here and controlled five of the major areas in the United States, was because one guy programmed all of those stations. We got a bunch of fans of his out here and we got a telegram with all these names on it, and we had the telegram blown up to the size of a double window that took a large truck to get it in. And then we had it delivered by United Parcel and it took two guys to carry it into the station. And the telegram says 'Please play *I Fought The Law*' with all these names on it and as big as the *Let Her Dance* record was as a follow-up, it was that much more difficult to get it on the number one station. I mean it was really tough, I gotta tell ya.. 'The Big Kahuna's in LA, hear all about it on KHJ', well that was our promotional gimmick."

Keene continues, "When we did the *Twist* albums, we used photographs of all the jockeys, which we didn't do on this one. Each station sent me their own photographs and we made up different covers each one. But that was more of a general promotion so that when they made something, they'd get on it for us. We had other things like we had a conference call that we instigated. We'd have maybe six or seven of the major stations and six or seven of the major cities across the United States and we'd have a conference call and they would all talk and say what's happening in their area. And then that would be recorded on tape and given it to *Billboard* and *Cashbox* and so on. I had a lot of those things going. As a west coast label, it was very difficult to get airplay on the east coast. I mean, I think we only got one or two records that I ever did that got big in New York City. And one of them of course was *Oldies But Goodies*, which was on another label and they took New York because they gave one record away for it. And at the time, I think my version with Little Caesar and the Romans was number nine and then they came out with it in New York. And of course Ritchie Valens did pretty well there. But we never—Alan Freed was out of the picture by the time Bobby Fuller came around, so we couldn't use him anymore. Dick Clark was… well, he played the record. But again, he was an east coast guy in those days. When I got Ritchie Valens and Little Caesar and some of my other acts on the Clark Show, it was a lot earlier in his career. It was back in the early sixties, or late fifties, and as time went on and on, Clark got more and more inaccessible. There were more and more deals being made under the table with different majors and stuff like that, so it cost you a fortune to get on the show, no matter what you had. We had to put stuff in that he had done in El Paso, because we didn't have enough cuts made yet. But the stuff made up in my studio, it was all of the same quality. We had to get an album out, so we took what we had."

"I didn't know they sang 'good fuck' in place of 'good fun' in *I Fought The Law*!" laughs Paul, "I'm not saying I wouldn't have

I FOUGHT THE LAW

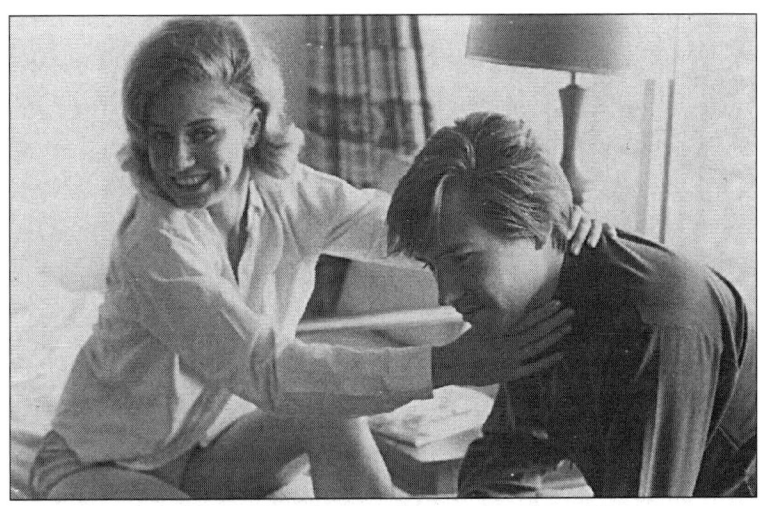

Bobby with unknown Georgia peach, 1966

used it if I had. It probably would've been a pretty good thing, but I didn't even know about it. *Ghost In The Invisible Bikini* we shot over in Pasadena. That was just a quickie cheapie, and again it was just a promotional gimmick. One reason why Del-Fi did so well, is because we were able to promote stuff. Yeah, we gave away hearses, you know, when we were promoting—we had a big stake in Pittsburgh because Clark Race, who was with KDKA back then, had a big thing going with this hearse, they had never seen a hearse like that before, where they had the surfboards, they had a big traffic jam with it in Pittsburgh. We'd run a contest in these cities where there was no water or anything, so surfing was completely—well, nobody knew anything about surfing in those days. In Pittsburgh, there was no water obviously. But we still ran our promo there and gave away a hearse to the winner, it was all run through the number one station in each city. And it caused a complete riot because they arrested Clark Race for holding up traffic and they had thousands and thousands of kids chasing this hearse down the main drag with the DJ and all this stuff. That was before Bobby."

I FOUGHT THE LAW

Keene: "The DJ's got off his record just like they did Ritchie Valens, because they wanted an established artist. And if you're not an established artist and you get killed, they don't want to play your record because you can't come in town and help promote it. And if you can't promote a record, then the DJs are using up time on the air with a record that'll never make it, and that's the kiss of death. That's how program directors get fired and all that kind of stuff. There's an unwritten law in radio that you cannot get on a record that's not gonna happen. That's why they're so hard to get going, because you have to prove yourself. It's a Catch 22, a record has to prove itself before it can get on an important station. So you gotta figure that if a guy had one big hit and he comes out with a second hit and it hasn't happened yet and he's been killed, they're gonna get off that record because they know damn well it's not gonna hit and they don't want to look bad. That's the way it goes and there are a lot of great artists that got buried because of that. Bobby Fuller was upset, he was ready to slash his wrists. I'm the guy that had the XKE and a Jaguar. I had the XKE and Bob-

LEFT: *Randy in Madras;*
RIGHT: *Girls with Bobby and Dalton, 1966*

by used to drive it. I also had a Shelby Ford, you know a hot rod Ford, and I let Bobby use that a lot, too."

"The basis of the record industry, especially in those days, was getting jockeys on your side," he continues, "because if you couldn't get on the air, they didn't care *how* great your record was. Fact, all the payola and all that other stuff, that's what it was all about. And it was the only way to get your records out there, even an order from a store, is to have it on the radio. I worked as a clarinetist for Frankie Laine, when he first came out here, before he was anybody. That's what you had to do. You had to get him on anywhere doing anything to try to get him going. Well, with Bobby, there were no club gigs in L.A. Casey Kasem was a disc jockey on a local radio station and he liked them and they did things for him, which was the way we worked. And hey, we had a going rate, working with the jockeys."

Keene: "Bobby's problem was that he didn't want to do anything other than sound like Buddy Holly. He was a purist, and I said, 'Look, don't copy Buddy Holly, the guy's dead and he's already a big hero, and what the hell, you'll only come out second best. Why don't you be Bobby Fuller?' So when we got the studio finished, we had the great chambers that I had designed and come up with the idea of putting them in tandem with the new board that we had. We had one of the first eight-tracks in town, as a matter of fact. It was all transistorized—I don't know any other one that was available. We could do things on it that other people couldn't do. And we could take these chambers and move them around, in tandem or place them in different spots in the program and get different sounds. But he didn't want any of that echo stuff, he wanted everything to be dry, and I said, 'Forget it.' Oh, yes. I mean we fought over that, and that was my whole concept of *Let Her Dance*, was to have that thing really swinging and charging through there, and he said something about that little *chink-chink-chink*, that was a Coke bottle that I had him hit, and he bitched about that. And you know, it was difficult to record because he didn't want to come up with anything new. He wanted to go and just do old stuff, and I said, 'Look, we want a new sound.' So that's how all that stuff came about, and Jim Reese had said later on that he was so upset that he came in and changed the mix at midnight while I wasn't there and all that kind of stuff. Well that's all a lot of crap because those studios were closed and on an alarm system and the whole thing. Nobody came in there at night while I was there, except maybe after Bobby was killed, and then Randy came in with his group and I let them go in and record. But the thing is, that from the standpoint of recording and so on, and *I Fought The Law* was the same way, he didn't want all the echo. I'd heard his record on *I Fought The Law*, and it wasn't any good at all, it was not a good record. We started from scratch, doing a whole new thing on it. Once we had gotten the sound on *Let Her Dance*, then that sound, I thought, would be a great commercial sound for Bobby. And putting that guitar—we put the acoustic guitar underneath everything—just a chunky kind of double time thing under there, gave it a lot of excitement, and we mixed it way back in the track just to give it that bad... you know like how Motown used to put everything but the kitchen sink on those tracks, and then they'd just move it back and back and back until there was just a *hint* of something there. And uh, of course that was completely contrary to his whole concept of Buddy Holly. But anyway, I feel I had a lot to do with the excitement of the record. *Let Her Dance* came out well, so that's really where we got the *I Fought The Law* sound. Jim Reese, to me, was kind of a bummer. He was always bitching about something, and he was

I FOUGHT THE LAW

LEFT: *Bobby and fans, 1966;*
RIGHT: *Bobby and Jeannie Romersheuser, 1966*

always complaining. He was a complainer. A real downer, the guy was. I never even thought he should been in the band, he didn't play that good, number one. And uh, I didn't know what the hell he was doing there. He didn't look good, he always had a sour look on his face. Anyway, I didn't like him and I guess he knew that, so that's why he said a lot of things about me. Jim always played rhythm guitar, except on *I Fought The Law*. The Bobby Fuller sound was something that I wanted him to do, which he didn't really want to do. They were all tough to work with, especially Bobby. He was so dedicated to, so adamant about what he wanted to do musically, and it was all along the Buddy Holly track. And of course when Barry White came in, he was completely the opposite, he was R&B and all that stuff. He didn't have anything to do with ever producing the Bobby Fuller stuff, but he *worked* for me. Barry White was an A&R man and worked in the office, so occasionally I would ask him something. He would've gotten producer credits, believe me! He was that kind of a guy. Barry White was never in the studio with Bobby Fuller. He was there a couple of times when we were just doing basics, but there was no instruction from him. They didn't *like* Barry White. They didn't like him at all. I may

LEFT: *Randy with Arlene Coletti, NYC 1966;*
RIGHT: *Randy Fuller Four 1967*

have asked Barry, like, what do you think about this idea or about that, and he may have said something, but I wouldn't say it to those Texans because they would have resented it."

Bob Keene was seriously taken with crossover advertising, and supremely attentive to the power of radio, and the burgeoning television teen show scene. It seemed that everywhere, there was a favor, a jingle, a tie-in, that needed doing in order to get radio play or television appearances. The first Bobby Fuller album was released on the heels of the *I Fought The Law* single in October of 1965.

"*King Of The Wheels* was a promotional thing that we worked out to get the guys going locally here," says Keene. "I had planned to put out like *The Twist* record, where we had put it out on twelve major radio stations in twelve different cities around the country. We planned to do that, twelve different covers and stations, with *King Of The Wheels*, but we never got around to it. In those days, it was about getting jockeys on your side, because if you couldn't get on the air, they didn't care *how* great your record was. Fact is, all the payola and all that other stuff, that's what it was all about."

The ad ploy may have worked locally with one station, but the album got no play anywhere on any station except KRLA—

and why should any radio station or disc jockey promote their competition. For an album as solid as *King Of The Wheels*, which read like a *Best Of The Bobby Fuller Four* with three stellar hotrod numbers added, to be presented like a K-TEL bargain LP was bad planning indeed, an error that was rectified with the *I Fought The Law* album four months later. But local push for *Wheels* was indeed effective.

Joyce Granville, a fan who first saw the Four in '65 recalls, "One of the wildest shows they ever did was at the Teen Age Fair at the Palladium. The Fair was an annual thing that went on for several weeks and bands would play, and they'd have slot car races and booths for musical instruments and teen fashions and all. Well, the Four were playing and they started throwing out copies of KRLA *King Of The Wheels* and the kids went nuts! People were going insane, tearing Bobby's clothes off! They took his belt and popped all the buttons off his shirt and someone in the crowd managed to grab him before the kids got his pants off entirely! Me and my friend Charlene were waiting for Bobby back at his apartment when he got back and he was so happy! He couldn't believe everybody liked him so much. I remember him laughing, 'THEY TOOK MY BELT!'"

Bobby added a surfers cross medallion to his daily wear, which he hung over his shirt and necktie, even when a cravat was called for. The cross was his badge of courage against the British Invasion—moptop mayhem would stick in Bobby's craw until his dying day. He knew that his band was not one of the thousands of new stateside combos that had sprung up in the wake of the Beatlemania, and he never took any element of the Merseybeat sound. Even when covering an occasional Beatles song at a teen dance at someone's behest, he would give it the Fuller treatment. His own sound, after all, had come together independent of any but American influences, and he was proud of it. Beatle George Harrison is quoted as saying that the Bobby Fuller Four was his most listened-to group in an early 1966 interview.

Jim Reese recalls one particular unpleasant, episode with an English band on tour in the States. "The Kinks came in to tape after us and a bunch of these girls came running up and told us that so-and-so from the Kinks had said that the Bobby Fuller Four look like a bunch of queers," said Jim, "so we sent in a message to tell them to come out and we'd show them what queers we were! We were gonna fold 'em up double and put 'em in a suitcase and send 'em back to England if they were gonna talk to us Texas boys that way!" This June '65 Kinks tour got them banned in the States for several years following—and Dave Davies told John Mendelssohn in *Kinks Kronikles*, "Other bands used to attract female groupies. The only people who ever came backstage were guys. A lot of people used to comment on how amusing it was to see so many guys backstage after a gig." So... the Kinks ought not to have talked! While on topic with of that brand of sensitivity, drummer Dewayne Quirico had his name changed because some disc jockey mispronounced his name as 'Queer-ico' (it's actually 'Care-i-ko'). For a short while thereafter, he was the easily pronounced Dewayne *Bryant*.

Blowouts continued, including a Disneyland Fantasyland Theatre blast, which featured a possibly psychedelicized Bobby Fuller pulling off three shows between 8 PM and midnight. "I really think he was doing acid at those Disneyland shows," recalled Jim. "He was acting real, real weird and we had to help him around after the shows." Well, leave it to Bobby to match substance with situation! Joyce Granville recalls hanging out at Bobby's apartment, when a teen talk show came over local radio. She listened to the hour-long broadcast with Bobby, who was

I FOUGHT THE LAW

very interested in what everybody was saying, as the show was about LSD. "He told me that he had tried it a couple of times and that all he ended up doing one time was sitting alone twisting a coat hanger into weird shapes!" she laughed. "I think he was just a curious person who wanted to experience everything."

The end of August featured a big party at the revered and rockin' Rendezvous Ballroom. Now by this time they were also booked to play DJ Dick Biondi's road shows. Jim describes those gigs, "The road shows were all high school dances. It seemed like every day for five or six months we were playing these local junior high and high school free shows during assembly periods. Dick had a bunch of bands on the shows and we never really knew who else was playing any of the shows because we were getting shuttled around so much. It was kinda crazy!"

The band has also been picked to perform in the A.I.P. movie *Bikini Party In A Haunted House*, which was renamed *The Ghost In The Invisible Bikini*. Jim describes the experience. "We never did understand why we couldn't do our own songs. All we

LEFT: *17 Magazine spread, 1966;*
RIGHT: *Thousand Oaks, last show for the BF4*

I FOUGHT THE LAW

did was go in and lip synch on the soundtrack that somebody else had recorded. Plus consider the fact that it was the first time we'd heard the songs, and here we were trying to lip synch on camera! On a couple of the songs, *Make The Music Pretty* and *Geronimo*, we went in later and put down vocal tracks, but we didn't play any of the instruments. In fact, we turned up on the set with our own guitars and amps and drums and stuff and they just took everything away from us and said we'd have to use the stuff they had there and it was all Vox equipment and we all HATED Vox stuff—basically it's good for one thing—starting bonfires! So it was real humiliating playing that crap, plus on the set they had one guitar, a bass, drums, and... a Vox organ! Well, guess who got to play the organ—*me*. So here I was, real proud of being a guitar player and all and they stick me behind an organ, and I'm supposed to act like I'm playing along to this terrible stuff! Wow! It was pretty bad. I never figured out why they had us play that Vox stuff until a couple of years ago when I saw that Vox promotional ad and there it was—a picture of us playing that crap in the movie! I mean it suggests that we actually played Vox equipment and God! We'd NEVER have touched the stuff in real life! I know for a fact that Bobby considered it

LEFT: *Bobby snoozes at Sycamore apartment;*
RIGHT: *Back stage with the Four, 1966*

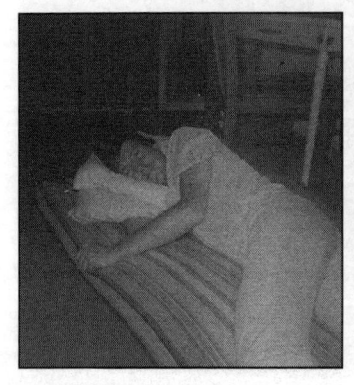

cheap stuff, and he was embarrassed to be seen with it. Back then we never knew they were gonna use it to endorse the product. I mean they could've asked us. We would've said NO!"

Dewayne claims that being in the *Ghost* was one of the highlights of his career, and for a most unusual reason—He got to meet his hero Boris Karloff. Dewayne: "The greatest part about it is that I had an hour long conversation with Boris Karloff and it was just the *goddamnest*. He was just a wonderful man, and I'm talking and we're sitting, waiting for our shot. And you know, you just have to sit around and *wait* and you get tired just from being bored. So I'm talking to the man, and he's just a wonderful person, and you know what? I'm sittin' there and all of a sudden, about halfway through the conversation, I say to myself, I go, 'I'm actually talking to the *Frankenstein monster!*' It was something *mind-blowing*, to me. I mean, I was a kid when I grew up and watched these—Bela Lugosi... Boris Karloff... It was just incredible. And at the time, you don't usually *think* about that. Maybe later on. But at the time, I actually *did*, you know, really gleaning the meaningfulness of it, 'cause you know, he's a cool guy, but not really taking it in, not until halfway through the conversation, that he was the *Frankenstein monster*. 'Cause he was so far away from that in the way that he presented himself there. You know, he was a business guy, an actor, whatever. He's Indian, too, I didn't know that. I *think* he's Indian, I'm not sure. That whole movie thing was a pretty cool thing. Nancy Sinatra was cool, Claudia Martin, Dean Martin's daughter, Aaron Kincaid, and the hot looking girl. And then Tommy Kirk—he got busted and fired from Disneyland. He had a Disney contract and got caught smokin' pot, but he was the *neatest* guy. It was shot down in a Pasadena *mansion*, a *hundred room* mansion, up, right over the Rose Bowl, you could see the Rose Bowl from it. And they had a *twenty-four* acre *garden* on the side of the mountain. So you could walk these paths, and on these breaks, me and Tommy Kirk would go down there, and we walked these paths and go down, and they had little gazebos *way down* the side of the mountain. I mean, it was like, if you lived there, you could have breakfast and that whole side of that mountain was yours to have breakfast on. I mean, that's all I could imagine. You know, a servant brings you down breakfast as you're taking your morning walk and you show up at this table and it's got orange juice, it's all waitin' for you. Pasadena—that's where all that started out there. All the homes are just awesome. *Huge* mansions, I mean *huge*. Beverly Hills is kinda like it, but it came after that. They toned down the mansion thing and made a smaller house but made it look like a mansion. It's old money there, it's real old money. You don't mess around in Pasadena. You know, here we were, in a movie with *Boris Karloff!* We were still based at Carlton Way, and six months earlier, I'd felt like I was still in an embryo stage. I mean, *Bobby* wasn't, *I* was. I mean we didn't have any hits or nothin', and then we did *'Driving down to Malibu-u-u.'* You know, it was something Keene was putting on us, really. I think Bobby woulda taken anything at that point, just to get noticed. But I did *not* like the song. Actually, *that song* was the *cause* of the Bobby Fuller and the Fanatics becoming the Bobby Fuller Four. Christmas, I was at my mother's. I went to my mom's in Huntington Beach and then Bobby was shopping the stuff around, and then along comes an audition at Rendezvous Ballroom. And we get an audition, and we *get* it. Then there was all the TV stuff, rapidfire. One thing, we were never ever on Shindig—never. *Ever.* Ever. Ev-ver. We were on *Shivaree, Lloyd Thaxton, Hollywood A Go-Go, Hullaballoo*. They were on *Action*, but that was with Dalton. Everything was happening real quick, and we did the Rendezvous Ballroom thing, and then we went from there, 'cause like I said, we were playing out there, and then Keene got us an audition at the Ambassador Hotel. We actually auditioned in the *big room* at the Ambassador Hotel. The most fondest memory I have of us there, other than playing there and the things that went on during us playing there is that one night, I'm standing there, hanging out in the hall, and *Charlie Watts* and Mick Jagger walked up to me and ask, 'Do you know where the lobby is?' 'Cause we were downstairs and you gotta go upstairs to go to the lobby in the hotel. And these were such Cockney accents, I didn't have no fuckin' idea what he was saying. I swear to you, it's just way more than just an English accent. And the reason they were at the Ambassador Hotel that night? Because they were coming in to town, and everybody knew what hotel they were gonna be at, and they switched it to the Ambassador. And they snuck them in there and there was no trouble."

Dewayne continues, "My sister was a go-go dancer at La Cave Pigalle. Bob Keene bought her go-go outfits! Swear to God. She would dance right beside us in a little box wearing a little fringy outfit, red and white, I think. And they had the little dangles that went *all the way up*, because when she moved, they flittered in that little go-go box. Just like Whisky A-Go-Go, only they had 'em in cages. It's unbelievable, really, and then we went from that and then we went to PJ's. My sister was a good dancer, she really was. I can tell you the girl who was there before her was Shelly Bonas, and Shelly Bonas used to go with Richard Pryor. Shelly Bonas' father got us on *The Danny Kaye Show*. We were on it in silhouette backing Shelly Bonas doing *Land Of A Thousand Dances*. We're *silhouetted*. And she's out there doing her go-go thing. And it aired—our first TV appearance. Only you couldn't see us! Swear to God. She had an afghan dog and she got us a gig on CBS. That's where I first met another real hot-looking chick—Julie Newmar!"

Jim recalled meeting Phil there: "Phil Spector never said much of anything except, 'Hey, how are you?' I remember we were glad he was interested in the band, but the way that Spector records people and the sound he likes to get wasn't what we were after. We didn't feel his sound and our music would be compatible. See, Bobby didn't even see eye-to-eye with Bob Keene about the way we were getting recorded and all that, let alone somebody like Phil Spector. I gotta say that we did get a lot of say in how our recording was done, considering. Nobody turned a deaf ear on us. We'd try things and if they didn't work, we'd try something else."

LEFT: *Girls with six guns, and Bobby;* RIGHT: *April Stevens and Nino Tempo with Bobby and Lord Tim, 1966*

CHAPTER THIRTEEN

THE MAGIC TOUCH
Coast-to-coast rock and roll—if this is fun,
why's it feel more like tragic, baby?

Paul Raffles had approached Bob Keene about having the BF4 record a live album at PJ's, as the Standells and others had done. Paul Politi and umpteen card carrying BF4 fans would agree that no matter how great the group was on record, nothing could compare to hearing them live in person. The idea of getting their incredible live performance sound onto a record was exciting. The original November 19 date for *Celebrity Night At PJ's* was rescheduled to December 3, as Bobby was hospitalized for a tonsillectomy before Thanksgiving. Always the professional, Bobby assured reporters after surgery, and right before the show, "I sing better than ever now." A list of teen appeal TV stars were in attendance at PJ's, including Lee Majors of *The Big Valley*, Ryan O'Neal from *Peyton Place*, Brenda Benet of *The Young Marrieds*, Meredith McRae of *Petticoat Junction*, and Sally Field of *Gidget*. The album was shelved due to technical issues. "The quality was substandard due to some problem," remembers Rick Stone, who was not at the show himself. "Bobby was super disappointed and told me that they were discussing the possibility of using bits from the show, like the talk between songs and the audience reaction and mixing it with studio recordings to make a fake live album. There had been an issue with the microphones and there was no way to get a decent album out of it." Keene was determined to get a second album out immediately to cash in on the chart success of *I Fought The Law*. The band doubled up the work attack in the studio plus kept up with a heavy load of local bookings. Despite the PJ's live album debacle, the 1965 holiday season was vastly different from the lonely, bleak holiday that Bobby had experienced the previous Christmas. In one year, the band had become a popular local act, and their headlining gig for New Years Eve at the all-new It's Boss teen club was one hot ticket. Young fan Joyce Granville was there: "They were great, as usual. The best thing about that night was that Bobby gave me and my friend Charlene a ride home after the show and kissed each of us goodnight. It was pretty thrilling!"

It's Boss was the famous old Ciro's night club at 8433 Sunset Boulevard that had gone bankrupt in 1959, thereafter renamed Ciro's Le Disc. By 1965, it was hosting the likes of Dick Dale and the Del-Tones and the Byrds. The club was purchased at the end of 1965 by Paul Raffles of PJ's, who turned named it, redecorated it (he commissioned Art Fine to produce huge pop art paintings especially for the club), and even co-wrote a theme song that he wanted the Bobby Fuller Four to record— *You spell it with an 'I' next is a 'T' and here comes the 'S' watch out for the B-O-S-S!* This was a bona fide teenager's club; if you were fifteen and a half, you could pay to enter. "Yeah. It was built for us. We were told," says Randy. "It was because they wanted us to play to the young audiences, too. They asked us to write a song about it and everything, but then they wrote it themselves. We were supposed to record that but I don't think we ever did. We only played at It's Boss and Gazzaris. The Bob-

I FOUGHT THE LAW

by Fuller Four never played the Whisky-A-Go-Go."

Bobby and the band were thrilled to play the opening night at It's Boss. It was a great way to swing into 1966. But the top teen roost was not theirs to enjoy for long, though, as Stereo Fi's Stars Of Tomorrow, working with GAC Talent, had sketched out a three month promotional tour for the BF4 in support of the *I Fought The Law* album and *Ghost In The Invisible Bikini* movie. The Four would spend April through June of 1966 crisscrossing the country, effectively removing themselves from an exploding LA music scene. For Bobby, it was daunting not to be hands-on with his career, as he enjoyed the behind-the-scenes work in the music business as much as he dug performing on stage. He had never liked being on the road for long stretches though, and this tour would prove to be grueling for him.

Dewayne Quirico had departed the Four soon after Celebrity Night, replaced by Bobby's old El Paso drummer friend Dalton Powell. One of Dewayne's last big shows had been on November 23 at the Carousel in West Covina with the Dave

I FOUGHT THE LAW

LEFT: *Bobby Fuller Four 1966;*
RIGHT: *Bobby is oblivious to his odd get up*

Clark Five and the Great Scots. Dewayne recalls, "Okay, we were talking about me basically getting fired. That would probably be the right word to use. I didn't really care. I cared, but I didn't care. I had started hanging out with Michael Clarke of the Byrds. We just hung out and got messed up together. I met a lot of interesting people. You have to hang with the people you're gonna be doing things with in this business. I went to PJ's one night, looking kinda rough-shaven. But I was actually feeling real good and walked in, I think I was doing some sessions or something, but I went to see the band, to see how they sounded since Dalton had come in. It was kind of shaky, but I could understand that. And so I came back in and Bobby calls me up to sit in, and we did *I Fought The Law*, and all the songs that we knew, that Dalton didn't know, and the crowd went crazy. They were glad I was there. And that made me feel cool. But it didn't make me want to be back with the band. I mean, it really didn't. I was more interested in a different kind of music. I wanted to be a session drummer, I wanted to learn everything."

Bob Keene's personal life was getting out of control. He describes his 44th birthday party in January '66 in a proof draft of his memoir: "…the party progressed. Inhibitions faded.

The guests started to loosen up and things began to get a little wild. One guest, a girl, had drunk too much or taken too many pills, and she had passed out in one of the downstairs bedrooms, which was readily accessible to anyone. In the downstairs poolroom, another couple were enjoying themselves on the pool table." He continues, "Sometimes I'd come home from the office and find bodies lying around semi-conscious, like you'd see in an opium den." He tells of going to a halfway house where treatment consisted of "getting as many shots of speed as one could afford in a day." He admits he "foolishly succumbed one day and joined them (meaning his wife Elsa and her sister) at the halfway house to try a shot of speed. I shall never forget the feeling of euphoria and well being that came over me… that wasn't the end of my shooting up. I continued the practice for a month. I was getting hooked."

Randy was unaware of any of this. To him, Bob was an older guy, a business guy, the person they had entrusted their future to. As far as the band knew, Keene was focused on all things Mustang, all thing Bobby Fuller Four. The distractions in Keene's private life might explain the five month lull in BF4 recordings and releases.

Before the start of the tour, the BF4 banged through a barrage of southern California shows, big and small, working Dalton into the fold. On February 12, they headlined the 7th Annual KFXM March Of Dimes Show at the Swing Auditorium, with Dick Dale and the Del-Tones, Jewel Akens, Cannibal and the Headhunters, the Bush, the Premiers, the Wattt Four, the Rumblers, the California Sons, and April and Nino. A show at the San Leandro Roller Arena on Friday the 18th and a Redwood City American Legion Hall teen hop on the 19th were followed by a Birmingham High School dance with disc jockey Dick Biondi on the 23rd. Thursday March 12 was a big homecoming dance in El Paso, at the Coliseum. Local press had given the Four a great build up, yet the turnout failed to impress. In the fourteen months that they had been in California, they had set the west coast afire, had been on TV numerous times, had made records and now had been the featured musical act in a movie, so why was coming back to the old stomping grounds suddenly a let down? Had they outgrown Texas, or was this another case of *I Can Never Go Home Any More*? By March 18 they were out west again, and kicking up sand at the Venice Youth Center.

Bob Keene's new hype on the group further served only to further remove them from the rock and roll mold that they had sprung from. "The Bobby Fuller Four have brought back, along with Herb Alpert and the New Christy Minstrels among others, an all-American look and sound to pop music," said Keene, who went on to tag the group's sound as "New-Country." Keene separating the BF4 from the burgeoning flock of shaggy, loud rock and roll bands on the Strip, by outfitting them in matching tricot outfits and keeping their locks shorn, set them apart from the bands they admired on the scene. Their promotion was better suited for either a young adult nightclub act destined for Las Vegas, or for a teen set chart-action group. Both angles effectively blurred the very clear vision that Bobby had for his own career. Bobby Fuller was a rock and roller. Meanwhile, Randy's ire was growing with every new dress code enforcement. He appealed to the fans via a column in the local teen tabloid *The Beat*, "If you girls would like him to wear his hair long and combed forward, perhaps you could convince Mr. Keene by writing a little note suggesting same." When Bobby was asked his opinion about hair in the same column, he avoided the subject with, "We put a tarantula in the elevator of our apartment building." The new pad was at

I FOUGHT THE LAW

LEFT: *Randy, 1966;*
RIGHT: *Bobby, last studio photo 1966*

1776 Sycamore, just around the corner and down a block from Grauman's Chinese Theatre, with a view of the Capitol Tower building for inspiration. It was a motel-style complex with a swimming pool, a courtyard, swinging young neighbors, and a place to park out back. There would be little time to enjoy the new digs, though, as a big national tour was set to begin the first week of April.

The Four kicked off the first leg of the junket on April 9 in Grand Rapids, Michigan, flying in from Los Angeles to meet up with newly appointed road manager Rick Stone, Bobby's sometime co-writer Mary Stone's son, whose first task had been to drive a van full of guitars, amps and drums two thousand miles north, as the crow flies. Rick picked the band up at the airport and as they headed into town, the saw a roadside drive-in theatre sign glowing: *The Ghost In The Invisible Bikini.* "We were all charged up about it," says Rick, who promptly turned the van right up to the entrance. "I told the guy at the ticket window that I had the Bobby Fuller Four with me and he didn't believe me so Bobby and the guys started singing *I Fought The*

I FOUGHT THE LAW

Law. The kid flipped and let us right in!" That night's Michigan show and dance was the first time any of them had been in the midwest and they were glad to see that their fans were singing along to the words and asking for autographs and pictures.

Next stop for the Four was the east coast. They were scheduled to play the Gene Kaye Show in Philadelphia but ended up instead with "the Geator with the Heater", DJ Jerry Blavat, who recalled having a blast with the Four. "Those guys had so much talent, so much going for them," says Jerry, adding with a pause, "I wonder... what happened to them?" A dance in South Amboy never materialized and instead, the first leg of the tour took them back west through New Jersey with DJ Gene Kaye back in tow, as he ran a circuit of dances in Philly, Bethlehem, and Allentown. They played his hop at Notre Dame Bandstand at Notre Dame High School in Bethlehem, and at Castle Rock at Dorney Park, Allentown, before heading to Pittsburgh to play with the Shangri-Las. Farther inland, they played Cleveland, Detroit and Chicago, all the while drawing great crowds with the success of *I Fought The Law* and also with *Love's Made*

LEFT: *Nancy Norton, NYC 1966;*
RIGHT: *Fun with fans at Sycamore apartment*

A Fool Of You which were starting to dent the Midwest charts. Local television appearances included a live performance on the *Jerry G. & Co* dance party TV show in Cleveland. The Chicago blast was at Dick Clark's Teen Fair, held outdoors in the old stockyards. It was pouring rain, but the show went on. Due to a booking error, they ended up the following night in LaCrosse, Wisconsin instead of Madison, and the band did not find out about it until they were in the wrong town. "Bobby ran down and found me having the truck worked on in a welding shop and we just tore out of there," said Rick. "We zigzagged all through this construction that was going on down town, and managed to drive that hundred and fifty mile trip in record time. We pulled up around ten o'clock—real late. We got out of the truck and it was raining, and we were all in bad moods and suddenly there are these football players—6′6″, 6′10″, and weighin' about 300 pounds apiece—comin' at us sayin' 'You're late and we're pissed off so you guys better be good or else we'll kick your butts!' Then one of the guys says, 'Yeah, the Turtles played here last week and they sucked! Y'all better play better'n they did or we are gonna kick your butts!' I was trying desperately to get the gear unloaded so I yelled 'Well, if you want us to play, come help us,' and this guy comes up and pushes me out of the way and he picks up this PA speaker that took two of us to carry and another guy took another speaker and they walked through the crowd with 'em over their heads! We were set up and the band was playing in 20 minutes! Bobby hit those big chords of *Peggy Sue* and they were amazing. Yeah, it was the most amazing gig the Bobby Fuller Four ever played. One five-minute break was all they took. It was something else. They played past curfew and the kids loved 'em."

Again, the guys hightailed it east, this time into New York City, skyscrapers and everything. They were booked for a two

I FOUGHT THE LAW

week engagement starting May 2nd at a trendy new nightclub called Ondine, 308 East 59th Street, which had just opened on April 16 with the Remains on tap. It would quickly become a favorite with the Warhol crowd- legend places Jim Morrison of the Doors here, gazing upon Gerard Malanga's leather pants, and drawing inspiration for his own more sophisticated wardrobe. Ondine was one of a big rash of new discotheques in NYC, which included Sybil Burton's jet set hangout Arthur, the Downtown, Trude Heller's, Clay Cole's, Scott Muni's Rolling Stone, Harlow's, the Phone Booth, the Happiness (Hong Kong-style!), the Cheetah, and Murray The K's World at Roosevelt Field, Long Island. During their New York stay, the BF4 were photographed for a fashion layout in *Seventeen* magazine with a bunch of pantsuit model chicks looking sternly arrogant. The interview that accompanied the spread had Bobby defending the band against the British Invasion, stating that they were doing Buddy Holly music years before they ever heard of the Beatles. He also claimed that his social life was "nowhere... I just like to play and write music. I go on a date once a month maybe." Bobby had, in fact, met a girl from Ohio at Ondine that week, a stewardess named Nancy Norton who took him around town to see the sights. The pair visited the UN and Cleopatra's Needle at the Metropolitan Museum of Art. Despite the many diversions of the city, Bobby felt out of place, and just one week out on the road, he was beginning to worry about what was happening with his career.

Bobby visited John Kurland at Ivor Associates on 55th Street while he was in New York. IA was handling publicity for the Four, and their April press release revealed an upcoming English tour, to commence after the Ondine residency. London Records had acquired the overseas rights to *Let Her Dance* and believed that the record and group could do very well overseas. Bob Keene had flown in, and spent several days visiting the offices of various record labels. One stop was at Roulette, Mustang's new sales chief Ron Roessler's previous employer. Aside from hearing a bit about Ron being from New York, Bobby had no idea that there was anything further brewing between Roulette and the gang on Selma. Roessler had suggested they check in with Charlie Koppelman at Char-Don Publishing for possible material for Bobby to record. There, they were pitched several songs, including *The Magic Touch*, which was recorded as a demo by Melba Moore. It was written by Ted Daryll whose *He Cried* was hitting by the Shangri-Las. The band was none to happy seeing Bob Keene staying at a swank hotel during his New York stay. They calmed down when he left for the Coast.

Meanwhile, teen TV host Clay Cole featured the band on his Saturday, May 14 broadcast with the Toys, Rare Breed, Percy Sledge, and Linda Scott. The next day, they played a Sunday afternoon high school hop in Brooklyn with local combos the Dematrons and the Esquires. Clay also got the guys on a show a Palisades Park, marking the start of a northern swing for the group, a trek that ended up taking them into upstate New York, New Hampshire (at Nashua's Go-Go Den), Massachusetts, Rhode Island and finally Portland, Maine. Rick recalls some of the shows. "They played a debutante ball at a place called the Country Club," said Rick. "It was like the oldest club in the United States, real uppity. All these rich people who could've cared less who was playing. That kind of thing always bugged Bobby. Anyway, after the show, we all were ticked off at the attitude there—I mean people wouldn't even clap or anything and the band was putting on a helluva show. There were still a lot of people left in there when we left. Randell had one of his homemade bombs, he was pissed—this thing was like a quarter stick of dynamite and so he left it under the porch with a slow fuse. I told him, 'Randell, you know you're gonna blow that whole damn porch off!' This place was a beautiful mansion. We drove out and watched those people and the funny thing is they were pointing at us wondering why we were just sitting there! Man, when that thing went off, it near lifted the place off the ground. Also while in Massachusetts, near the Kennedy compound, the band's van got nailed by the Highway Patrol because it had an expired temporary California sticker on it. "It's weird," laughs Rick. "They waited 'til we had all our instruments in the van and then they towed it. This guy John MacDonald who'd booked the gig for us, knew a guy who worked at the police garage where they took it so he left the gate open for us on Sunday night around 2 AM so we went and stole our van back outta the impound deal! It was incredibly foggy."

"We had to stay at John's place for a few days because the heat kept hanging around," says Randy. "That's why we left late at night. He took us around the area to clubs and shopping center's where we signed autographs. When we left he led us through the back roads to avoid the State Trooper."

"In Cambridge, Massachusetts some dyed-in-the-wool old agent who booked everything from boxing matches to marching bands got the guys a gig playing on a flatbed truck in the middle of nowhere on a Sunday afternoon between nightclub bookings," remembers Rick. "It was outside of Boston and very few people ever knew about it. But they played it, on the back of a truck out in the country. They really got some different type gigs—everything from big stadiums to gyms to… flatbed trucks!" While in New England, Rick recalls going with Bobby to some recording studios in Boston, just to check them out. Their agent on the east coast was also the Remains' agent, so they hung out with Barry and the guys whenever they were around.

I FOUGHT THE LAW

Bobby was a phone-in guest with Dick Clark on *Bandstand* while they were in the northeast. "We were sort of wondering if Dick Clark was really going to call," says Rick, "but then the phone rang and it was him and Bobby was real cool, talking to Dick, telling him about the tour and recording and all, and all the while Randell was lighting up another one of his bombs and right in the middle of this *Bandstand* conversation the flash bomb goes off, real bright and scary and old Bobby doesn't miss a beat, just keeps talking, just goes on cool as can be!"

Back in LA the Four started working on the new record, which Bob Keene wanted to put out immediately to coincide with the rest of the tour. Bobby was getting to answers to his inquiries about a British tour. Kurland at Ivor Associates, after all, had announced it. Keene avoided a direct response about it and told Bobby to focus on recording. Bobby did not like *Magic*, but had been hoping to give it the West Texas treatment and was trying desperately to maintain some control over the record. Contrary to previous accounts, Barry White had "nothing to do with the session" according to Bob Keene. "At that time, Barry was an A&R man in LA and he may have been at the studio when we were doing basic tracks for the record, but he never had anything to do with the production. Bobby was, and I can't say this enough, totally wrapped up in this Buddy Holly thing and of course Barry White represented something he disliked so in turn, he disliked Barry White. But Barry never had anything to do with production. He would've gotten production credits, believe me. He was that kind of guy!"

"Bobby was furious," says Rick. "Bobby hated that Motown thing they did to the song. He was real proud of his West Texas sound and could not understand why Keene had gone ahead on his own and made a major decision like this without his approval. He didn't like recording a song they couldn't duplicate live and *The Magic Touch* was overdub over overdub over overdub and they tried and tried to get it right live and it just sounded like hell. It didn't make any sense that a band would record a song they couldn't cut live."

The same sessions also produced *My True Love* (which Bobby had written with Mary Stone—she had wanted it to be a Nashville-type production) which became the B side to *Magic Touch* and two songs which were to remain unreleased for twenty years—*I'm A Lucky Guy* and the gorgeous *It's Love*,

I FOUGHT THE LAW

Come What May.

Jim Reese recalled the last session and the great fuzz-laden version of the supreme *Baby My Heart* which was taken from the same side of the *In Style With The Crickets* LP as *I Fought The Law* and *Love's Made A Fool Of You*! At the time, the Crickets recorded *In Style,* they were hanging around with the Everly Brothers and that influence shows all the way into the BF4 versions of the Crickets' songs, especially on *Baby My Heart.* "We used an empty beer bottle and a drumstick," explained Jim, recalling the percussion accent that threads through the song. About the fuzz tone effect, he added. "Bobby liked experimenting with anything new and different."

While the group was on tour, major changes were in the works back at Mustang. By March, Larry Nunes and Martin Goodman of Stereo Fi had joined forces with twenty year music biz veteran Norm Goodwin to form Privilege Distribution with offices at 2818 West Pico Boulevard in LA. In addition to partnership control at Stereo-Fi/Mustang, Nunes, Goodman, and now Goodwin, via Privilege, held worldwide rights to the Bobby Fuller Four and their recordings, and, in the western and southern states, for talent on independent labels including Monument, Hanna Barbera, Tower, GNP Crescendo, and Original Sound. The April 2, 1966 issue of *Billboard* described, in an understatement, an "aggressive sales state of mind" going on at Privilege.

Also in April, Ron Roessler, the sales chief at Morris Levy's Roulette Records in New York City, inexplicably arrived at Selma Avenue to become the general manager of Mustang to head up the sales department there. He would not have been lured away from Levy by Nunes because neither would have been interested in compromising the mega-million dollar deal that would wrap a month after Bobby Fuller's death, when a full-page *Billboard* ad announced that Nunes, Goodman and Goodwin were "proud to announce the signing of an exclusive contract with Roulette and Tico Records" via their monster new firm, ITCC (International Tape Cartridge Corporation), which was at the forefront of the new, portable 8-track and 4-track tape revolution. The negotiations for this union had been underway for months, with industry interest going wild about affordable automobile and otherwise portable music players, and an easily replicable format to play in the devices. ITCC was in place with unique plastics manufacturers to distribute millions of 8-track and 4-track tapes nationally and internationally.

From his new perch at Stereo-Fi, Roessler had the inside track on sales and other things pertaining to Mustang Records and its star, Bobby Fuller. There was one master that had been of interest to those in the east. *Let Her Dance* had almost died on the vine with the divisive movements of Mustang and Liberty. Had it enjoyed an uninterrupted push by either label, or by another, it would have charted much higher. Of this there can be no debate. By 1965, and certainly by the following year, the Frankie and Fabian style teenage heartthrobs had been curbed by the great rock and roll band takeover. Still, a dynamic front man, a solo artist with a cool backing combo and personality, was the easiest to promote. Lou Christie, Neil Diamond, Del Shannon and Tommy James are prime examples.

Tommy James entered the 1966 charts with *Hanky Panky* on June 2, less than a month after Roulette had acquired Jack Deafenbaugh's two and a half year old Snap label from Pittsburgh record pusher Ernie Kashauer and promoter Bob Mack. "The guy who played sax for Tommy, he quit because it was too *hectic* up there," says Kashauer, meaning New York City. "He was more of a mild mannered guy. He heard Nate McCalla say he'd take care of Bobby Fuller. Bobby had made a deal with

I FOUGHT THE LAW

LEFT: *Bobby Fuller is Mondo from his head to his feet;*
RIGHT: *Bobby in Brooklyn, 1966*

Morris Levy to sell his copyrights. At the last minute he backed up a bit. Supposedly, Morris gave him the money and Bobby Fuller didn't want to do it. Then Bobby Fuller was found dead. He supposedly swallowed gasoline. Morris also tried to get rid of Jimmie Rodgers. James Sheppard wanted his copyrights back from Morris and he was found dead. Frankie Lymon was found dead because he was going to see Morris about his copyright. I heard some of this myself when I was up at Roulette. Hank Ballard supposedly needed money and Morris bought the copyrights off him and Hank wanted this copyrights back and Morris said, 'No, no, no—keep it up and you're gonna go the route of the rest of these guys' and Hank backed off. I heard that from Hank Ballard himself. Morris had a bad habit of not paying royalties, I had a contract with him for twenty years. The only reason I got paid was that I was brought in by Nick Cenci and John La Rocca. John was head of the mob in Pittsburgh. Nick Cenci was real good friends with Morris Levy and he was also Roulette's distributor in Pittsburgh. Bobby Fuller most definitely met with Morris. You make a deal with Morris, that's it. You don't go back. Morris' enforcer Nate McCalla was murdered. He's the one who did the deeds and they found him in Florida with his throat cut. If you ever get a hold of Lloyd

Price, his manager was Harold Logan. He came up to see me and he walked in with Lloyd Price because I was distributing their Double L label. I found out that Logan had something to do with Morris' mob and they found him shot, He owed Morris money."

Tommy James said in his book *Me, The Mob, And The Music*, "It seems that once a month Morris would grab Nate McCalla and a few baseball bats, which were always in his office, and take off for somewhere in New Jersey or upstate New York. It was a ritual. Nate fought in Korea. He was a decorated hero. He said, 'Do you realize what the United States government taught me? They taught me to kill people, so that's what I do.' And he was serious."

New York's Richard Manzi's recollections support Kashauer's story, "I had accessibility to Morris Levy. My dad was involved with him and it made it much easier for the door to be opened. I was hanging around at many different record labels in New York. Laurie Records. Bob and Jean Schwartz, Eliot Greenberg and Ernie Maresca. I was a kid just hanging around, breaking balls looking for records and buying records, 'hey I wanna go in the studio', that kind of stuff. My parents insisted that I get an education. Here I was, in high school, making con artist deals with my teachers, asking for one day off a week so I could do some work, so every Thursday I wouldn't be in class. Then one day a week became two days and it went out of control. I was very close with the Laurie situation and once I got involved with Morris at Roulette, one day I go to Laurie Records and they say, 'no no no now you're Moishe's kid. No no Rick, go over there'. I was the go-fer—go for this, go for that. Go get coffee. He'd play demos for me and ask me what I thought of certain records, very openly because of the background I have. I'll let you read between the lines of that. The background that I was exposed to. It was nothing to walk into the office and see people like Chin Gigante, who twenty years later would be walking around in the Village in a bathrobe. Enough said. Other well-known people were involved with Levy. That was the problem with Roulette. There was so much money coming from organized crime. That something that I'm saying, that the police department, the federal task force, I've had access to documents. It was organized crime that kept Roulette above water. Back to James Sheppard. James was upset about royalties and he was hounding Morris about it, and that's once thing you couldn't do. James was a success with the Heartbeats, with Shep and the Limelites, he had influence over some of the younger performers. *Don't go fuckin' near Roulette. He's a thief. He'll sue your eyeballs out and that's a fact.* I heard that as a kid. That's one thing Morris Levy never liked to be called and that's a thief. He never liked thieves. He grew up in the Bronx with Chin Gigante. Grew up poor, on public assistance, I believe, a hard worker when he was young, worked as a photographer, a penny here a penny there. He may have respected certain Black people but he looked down on blacks, he thought they were low class, and that's putting it nicely. I heard him say, 'I'm not gonna give him money? What's he gonna do with it, buy a bottle of booze!' James Sheppard was found murdered in the street and his pockets weren't empty. When you get mugged in Jamaica Queens, there's not gonna be any money in your pockets. Here's another story that was confirmed. There was this guy Jimmie Rodgers. Back then, the word was that you don't leave Roulette. 'You get an offer from another label, I'll break your fuckin legs.' That's a quote. Jimmie Rodgers decides he's gonna take an offer from A&M Records. They found him in LA with his head bashed in. That was a hell of a message. That was the price you paid for leaving Roulette. Jimmie Rodgers was not a name you brought up in the office. You never brought up anything about James Sheppard. You never brought up anything about Bobby Fuller. I swear until the day I die, I swear on my parents' lives that I saw a copy of *Let Her Dance* in that office on Roulette, on a white promo label. I saw that copy and of course I wanted it. It's not listed in the Roulette discography. When I first went there, I'd go for coffee, he'd give me a fifty dollar bill. Sometimes he'd give me the money and tell me to go for coffee and not come back. Bobby Fuller came to the Roulette offices. My father loved him. I remember when the news came on that Bobby had been found dead. My father threw a chair full force into the TV set, cursing."

A listing of Roulette Records 45 RPM releases for 1965-1966 reveals two unassigned catalog numbers, #4635 in the summer 1965, and another, #4685 in mid-1966, immediately before Roulette #4685, *Hanky Panky*. Were these numbers pre-assigned for *Let Her Dance* to finally find its chart glory on Roulette?

At the end of May, the Four flew out to Atlanta to meet Rick for a series of Dixie dates with the Newbeats, Jimmy Gilmer and the Fireballs, and a fake Sir Douglas Quintet. Aside from being worried about leaving the new recordings behind half-baked, he was unhappy to be playing with the counterfeit SDQ

I FOUGHT THE LAW

as well. "Bobby was a big fan of Doug Sahm," recalls New York fan (and president of the Lou Christie Fan Club) Arlene Coletti, "I remember him talking about him a lot up in New York. If he didn't really know him, he spoke of him as though he did, you know, like he was a good friend who he thought a whole lot of." Travel in the southern states was hot, dirty and very hectic. The guys never got enough rest but they managed to survive the dates in Birmingham, Little Rock and Mobile, and the shows went well, judging from the massive amounts of fan mail Bobby received from the south. To break up the boredom of the long hauls between gigs, the guys turned to their love of fireworks, firecrackers and bombs. "I bought two cases of cherry bombs—M80's—down there and boy, did we have fun with 'em! We had a trap door in the floor of the van and we'd drop 'em down so they'd explode under a car behind us," recalled Rick. "It was great!" The bombing continued through the south, and it took an edge off the heat and hassles. They also enjoyed singing dirty lyrics to some of Bob Keene pop songs that he was always trying to impress them with.

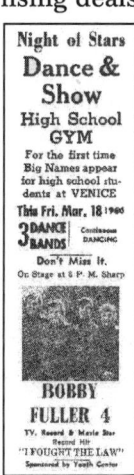

Keene had now confirmed a British tour for the Four in August, a fact that lifted Bobby's spirits a bit. Licensing deals were in place with London Records for singles, and he had just inked with President for the release of the *I Fought The Law* album, set to coincide, ideally, with the UK tour. Meanwhile, Morris Levy had signed with a British distributor, Radio Caroline's Irish co-director Phil Solomon's new Major Minor Records, which promptly propelled Levy's new hitmaker Tommy James to the top of the proverbial pops.

Music publisher Ed Kassner had launched President Records in England at the same time that Major Minor had hung out a shingle in 1966, on the heels of his US label of the same name, which between 1963-66, had issued rock n' roll which included Charlie Gracie and the Jodimars. Kassner's early strides in the music business had been in publishing and sheet music, with acquired copyrights on perennials including *Take Me Out To The Ball Game*, *You Made Me Love You*, and *Rock Around The Clock* (which he purchased for $250 in the mid-1950's). The label was one of a handful of British independents at the time, yet Kassner, having secured UK publishing rights for Chicago's VAPAC Music and Los Angeles based Maravilla, the publishing arm of Stereo-Fi Music/Mustang Records, was on the move by nailing down the publishing first. This had been the *modus operendi* of Morris Levy—copyrights first, everything else will follow. Supporting the deal were savvy master license agreements which launched a barrage of President 45's farmed from the US labels associated with the respective publishing firms. George and Ernie Leaner's One-Der-Ful/Mar-V-Lus label and Bob Keane's Mustang/Bronco soul stable were cherry picked for hits and the new President label was off and running.

President was perched to issue the *I Fought The Law* album to coincide with the the BF4 British tour, which never did transpire. Several months after Bobby's death, they did issue the LP as *The Bobby Fuller Memorial Album*.

The Magic Touch was quickly issued on Mustang, despite Bobby's anxieties. Rick had again driven up to New York and met the band at the TWA terminal at Kennedy Airport on June 9. "From the very start, things were off the mark for the second New York visit," said Rick. "First off, we had been booked into a hotel near the club and when we got there, they flipped when they saw we were a rock and roll band, and they said they didn't allow rock and roll bands, and here we go again, not knowing where to go, pounding the pavement to find a hotel. Unbelievable." The two-week stint at the Phone Booth at 152 East 55th Street turned out to be pretty much of a disaster. "The Cheetah Club had just opened that week and the crowds were all heading over to it to check it out. So the crowds at the Phone Booth weren't all that great. One night there was a bunch of GI's who came stumbling in and they started yelling 'Y'all sound like Buddy Holly! Play some Buddy Holly!' and Bobby and the guys played for two solid hours—every damn Buddy Holly, Eddie Cochran and Roy Orbison song they knew! The GI's and everybody else there was floored. There was just no comparison to Bobby Fuller on record and Bobby Fuller on stage at that time. You know that live version of *Miserlou* that's

I FOUGHT THE LAW

around? That's absolutely terrible compared to the way Bobby was playin' it the last six months he was alive, believe it or not. By that time his guitar playing was scorching. He'd gone from playing co-lead on some songs to playing the whole leads on almost everything. I wish tapes existed of those NY shows, because I tell you, they were incredible. Four shows a night for two weeks straight. That's forty-eight New York City shows!"

"I met the Bobby Fuller Four at their second appearance on *The Clay Cole Show*," said Arlene Coletti, who in 1966 had the Perfect Teenage Job as Cole's assistant on his local NY teen TV bash, *The Clay Cole Show*. "They were on Clay's show on June 25th with Eddie Rambeau, the Chosen Few, Baby Jane Holzer, and the Uncalled For Three! I went to all the Phone Booth shows," explained Arlene, "and they were all great! It was pretty unbelievable, because I was sixteen at the time and hanging around every day that they were here, with the Bobby Fuller Four. Bobby was sort of shy, and he was kind of like a brother type to me. His shows were phenomenal and a lot of fun. He was always hanging out with his fans, not a bit stuck up or

RIGHT: *On top of the world, 1966*

anything, I remember there was this English girl named Peggy who came to all the shows and I'd have to translate when she'd talk to Bobby. She had this real fast Liverpudlian accent and of course the Fullers had that slow Southern drawl! Bobby dedicated *Peggy Sue* to her and of course she loved it. He also sang *A New Shade Of Blue* to me every night! There was this time in the dressing room when a bunch of us—the Four and the opening act, a duo, I think, and me and Peggy—got into this game that Bobby had started up during their break. We were all there sitting in a circle on the floor and we'd have to sing the first two lines of a Buddy Holly song and whoever couldn't do it was out, so we went around and around and finally it was just me and Bobby and it was my turn and I couldn't think and then I sang out 'Little things you say and do...' and I looked at Bobby and he had this sick look on his face and I knew he was drawing a blank. He couldn't remember any more songs—I had beaten him at his own game! Later that night he came up to me, acting sort of nonchalant, and said, 'Hey, I thought you didn't know any Buddy Holly' and I said 'I don't! I just know the songs you play! I just happened to remember *Rave On!*' But he was still mad. The next night I went up to him and said, 'Wanna play again?' He went, '*no way!*' To this day, I have to smile and maybe shed a tear or two when I hear *Rave On*." Arlene went on to talk about Bobby, the person: "He was really a lot quieter than Randy. One time I went over to the hotel and I walked in his room and the lights were out and I was turning to go back out when I hear him call 'Arlene' and I looked around and I couldn't see him so he says 'follow the voice, follow the voice' and here he was sitting on the floor in a corner by the sofa so I asked 'what are you doing sitting in the dark?' and he said 'I'm sitting in the dark.' He was like that, introverted. But other times he was just as crazy as Randy, like when they were throwing watermelons at people from their hotel windows!"

Randy was continuing to have his pyromaniac brand of fun at the Phone Booth. "He'd hook cigarettes to those cherry bombs fuses so they'd made a slow burn and then he'd watch as they went off, at a safe distance!" said Jim, also recalling a Randy incident with Gloria Stavers, editor of the fabulous *16 Magazine*, who had caught the Four several times at Ondine, and had commented in the latest *16* that the BF4 had, "beat a path to Greenwich Village's swinging men's shop the Shed House" to shop and that Bobby favors a "weird combination of Mod and Western gear".

"Gloria was interviewing the guys and we were in a restaurant in an exclusive hotel and Randell and Dalton didn't have ties, which were required and the restaurant made them put on these like size 46 coats, you know, way too big. Man, it was too much! Anyway, Gloria and Randy were getting the hots for each other and it was turning into a Randy Fuller interview more than anything else. The two of them wanted to go to a nightclub so Dalton and Jim went back to sleep and Bob and I went to get some money out of our rooms. There was some kind of convention going on downstairs at the hotel so the lobby was crowded. Well, Randy and Gloria were supposed to meet us in the hotel bar and when we got down the stairs the whole place was like a parting of the people staring at us and I thought, 'Gee, all these people know Bobby Fuller already?' So the four of us get in a cab and we get around three blocks and Randy hits his hand with his fist and says, 'Boy, did I catch that son of a bitch!' And I said 'What?' And Gloria starts telling us how Randy had caught some guy looking at her, telling his friends 'Boy, would I like to...' and Randell had belted him good, cold-cocked him, *wham*, into the wall, and as Gloria described it, the guy had slid down the wall onto the floor real

slow like in the movies and then he'd kicked the guy in the face a few times. I said 'Man, that's bad!' and Gloria says, 'Not as bad as you! He hit the wrong guy!' We ended up staying out the whole night and when we got back to our rooms all the red lights were flashing on the phones! Man! Well, Bobby left some cash at the front desk for the guy who'd been clobbered and we cut out the back door!" The whole New York stop ended up infuriating Bobby and the band, as the manager of the Phone Booth refused to pay them at the end of the week, claiming their bar tab for two weeks was twenty-six hundred dollars. "Yeah, they charged us fourteen hundred dollars for corkage the first week and Bobby freaked out, 'cause like we got a discount on beer and drinks at the bar and each of us always paid cash for that. And the band never drank while they were onstage. I'd take up trays of ice water and that was it. They couldn't have bought more'n fifty bucks in beers at the bar all week and like I said, they'd always paid cash for 'em anyway. So Bobby had me—since I was the road manager—go see the owner, Sam Siegal and he THREW me up against the wall and then out the door with plenty of threats. One night when the crowd was real small they hired a topless go-go dancer without us knowing and Bobby was real upset but he didn't want to embarrass the girl so he didn't say anything to upset her, but that night he told Siegal that he wouldn't go on again if he ever did that to him again. One person who did show up at several shows was Ahmet Ertegun of Atlantic Records and though Bobby never did say anything to me about it, we all thought maybe Bob Keene was negotiating with him about Bobby's contract." Ertegun's Bang label was going strong with the Strangeloves and the McCoys, and the Bobby Fuller Four would've been a a good fit. Bobby was in a funk about the whole New York experience. "He just wanted to get the hell out of New York as soon as possible," says Rick. Arlene Coletti backed this up, "Bobby hated New York. He loved California, everything about it. He even complained about our orange juice because it came from Florida instead of California. According to Bobby everything was better if it was from out west."

Teenage hijinx and rock and roll fun aside, Daniel had turned to bicker within the Four, not unusual for four guys and a driver who had been on top of each other for nearly three

LEFT: *Bobby in El Paso 1966;*
RIGHT: *Post-Vitalis Randy*

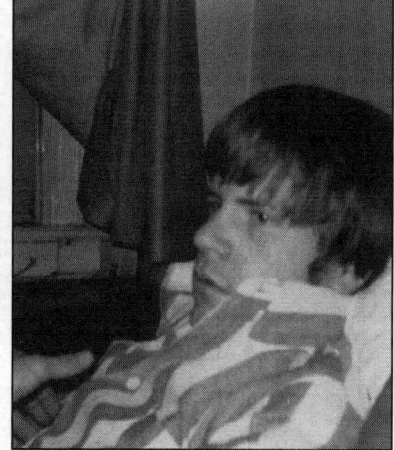

months running. Jim Reese felt that things had been changing within the band for some time. For one, he felt Keene was putting more and more emphasis on Bobby as a solo entertainer and that he was making the others feel slighted. Randy, of course, felt the same way, although Dalton, the short tenure member, was ambivalent.

The cherry bomb supply had been used up and the laughs grew few and far between. The radio in the Greenbrier kept tuning in *The Magic Touch*, which had just been released. This depressed Bobby to no end.

Rick drove five days with virtually no sleep, through Dallas, down and across to El Paso and then across the sands to LA. Once in town, the guys collapsed by the pool at 1776. The next gig was in San Francisco, where they were getting play on KYA 1260. The gig was at the Dragon A Go-Go, located in the basement of the Luo Wah Restaurant at 49 Wentworth Alley, formerly the Lions Den. It would be the last engagement for Bobby Fuller at the club that encouraged a clientele 'from eighteen to eighty'. Bobby would come away from the experience with one happy memory, that of hearing the Golliwogs *Brown Eyed Girl*. He would return to Los Angeles to recommend John Fogerty's pre-Creedence Clearwater Revival combo to Bob Keene. Aside from that, the trip was a total disaster. "We drove six hours straight to San Francisco to find that the club had done zero advertising. Things were really bad by now," recalls Rick. "One night Bobby and Randell had an out-and-out fist fight. The band played four nights to real small audiences and after the fourth night we just packed up to split and the owner comes flying out of the door going wild and threatening Bobby. We just said screw it and went home. Bob was real, real tired of it all. The whole band was."

Back in LA, Bobby was stony when he met with Bob Keene

I FOUGHT THE LAW

in an attempt to find out what exactly was happening behind the scenes at Mustang. The three months of touring had removed him from this new LA roost and had broken up the band. Rather than being able to spend time at home and in the studio working on his own material, he was being forced to record other songwriters' compositions. He didn't need an A&R guy. Bobby could do his own A&R'ing better than anybody else. He could also do his own promotion better. He felt misunderstood and abused. The positive response to *It's Love Come What May* served to buoy his spirits, and gave him some hope to regain his momentum, despite the fact that the band was crumbling. Dalton told everybody that he was going home to with his wife and family, and Jim Reese received his draft notice. The bickering was quieting down as everyone realized there was no point in fighting if breakup was inevitable. Although they were about to go their own ways, the Four planned to finish work on *Baby My Heart* and a few other cuts that they had half completed in the studio. They played what they all presumed to be "possibly, probably" their last show with Casey Kasem and Thousand Oaks. Ironically, they had played their first show on the coast there with Casey just a year and a half earlier. Jim Reese offered to sell Bobby his new XKE and Bobby said he'd think it over. Bobby was waiting to hear back from Pamela, who had told him that she needed time to think about joining him in California.

Rick Stone and two girls, who were in town from El Paso, were at Bobby's apartment talking and watching TV and drinking beer on the evening of July 17th. It was Sunday night. "Bobby had five or six beers himself and was feeling pretty good," said Rick. "The girls left at about 11:30 and Bobby went out at about 1 AM, saying he was going over to this chick Melody's place to buy some acid." Rick says he had been on a similar

Hanging out at Sycamore

LSD run to Mel's earlier that week with Bobby, and when Bob saw there was another car in her driveway beside her blue 1964 Cadillac Eldorado ragtop, he'd told Rick to peel out and keep going and that it was better if he came back some other time. Bobby returned to the apartment a couple of hours later and was working on a second six pack at the super's pad on the third floor. Bobby had a band meeting at 9:30. Does Rick's story seem likely—would Bobby have been drinking and partying before an important meeting? Were drugs even a part of the M.O.?

"I had fallen asleep watching TV after Bobby left and woke up around 2:30. I went in the kitchen to fix an ice tea and heard someone going out the front door, but I didn't see who it was—I figured it might've been Bob going out to the car or something. I didn't really stop to think about it. I just went to sleep again. The next morning Mrs. Fuller woke me, saying that Bobby hadn't come home yet. I went out to look for his car and it wasn't in the drive or in the garage. I wasn't worried at the time, figuring he'd just stayed out having a good time. We all had a meeting at Keene's office at 9:30 so I headed over there. Everybody else was there but when Bobby didn't turn

I FOUGHT THE LAW

up by 10:30, we rescheduled for 3:30. He still didn't turn up so I headed back to the apartment and that's when I saw all the police cars and they tried to stop me from going into the drive, 'cause I saw Bobby's car and I told them who I was and they let me through. Bobby was there lying in the car, all beat up real bad and gasoline all over him and there like burns on him—the cops said the gas had burned his skin in the heat. I knew he was dead. God, it was awful."

Ty Grimes and Mike Ciccarelli were already there when Rick arrived, having come by to visit, at about 5 PM. As they entered the apartment building to take the elevator up, they heard screaming out in the lot, and they hurried back out. Loraine had gone through the back corridor and down the back staircase to check for her car again, as she had been checking throughout the day. This time, she saw her blue Oldsmobile in the lot, and rushed over to it. When she opened the driver side door, she saw her son slumped, lifeless, in driver seat. She ran upstairs, terrified, to call the police. Ty and Mike were in total shock at the grisly sight. They noted dried blood on Bobby, and it appeared that he had been beaten and thrown into the car with what appeared, and smelled, to be gasoline thrown in over him. The gasoline smell was overpowering. By the time the police arrived, Rick Stone and neighbors had gathered to watch the coroners people pull the body out and shift it into a first call vehicle. Everyone present in the parking lot that afternoon saw Bobby's blistered, beaten frame, smelled and saw the gasoline, as well as a gas can on the floor of the passenger side. His slippers, according to Rick, were worn and dirty, as though he had been dragged.

Local newspapers splashed suicide stories the following day. When the police asked Loraine Fuller if her son had been depressed, she said yes, knowing that he was in a low mood about the band business that he had to deal with that morning. The police took that response at face value and promptly penciled in a suicide verdict. Bobby Fuller to them was just another rock and roll kid from out of town whose dreams had come crashing down around his head. It would take months to get a final formal death certificate and autopsy report, and a revision at that. But now, suddenly, a funeral had to be organized.

Wayne Ratliff was a pilot who flew for El Paso Natural Gas. He had just returned from an executive flight to South America when he was notified of Bobby Fuller's death and was called upon to fly Lawson Fuller from El Paso to Burbank Airport. Loraine was inconsolable, beyond devastated.

That afternoon, Rick was almost run off the road by a car that was following him in the Hollywood Hills. Everyone was on edge. Rick remembered being in the car a few days earlier, when a car with two men had pulled up, and beckoned for Bobby to come over. Rick stayed in the car while Bobby walked over, talked for a couple of minutes, and then came back, ash white and obviously shook up. He wouldn't talk about it. "Rick

Bobby is chatty and hungry, 1966

I FOUGHT THE LAW

Stone told me that Jim and Dalton said two guys tried to break into their place and had guns," said Randell, "and he said, 'Come on, let's go try to find them.' And man, I drove the car and we drove around looking for these guys. Bob Keene acted like he didn't really care. He was losing his business, and so that's probably why he didn't really care about Bobby or us. And Larry Nunes didn't care because he had his business and all. And now he had Barry White. Keene lost his studio right after Bobby died. All I know is that it was Bob Keene who said we were having to have life insurance. The band had one separate from Bobby. And for Bobby, it was a lot of money. I think we weren't near as much. But there were insurance policies, and Bob Keene was the one that we were signing with at that time. And that might've been before Nunes even came into the picture."

Dewayne was playing in a club in North Hollywood with Chuck and Joel and the Trippers that night. "My wife called me and said, 'Did you know that Bobby died today?' And I go, 'No way,' and I finished the gig and went home," says Dewayne. The next day I tried to call, but Randell was just real distraught about it, and so I just stayed put. Then there was a big investigation going on and this rumor about him being murdered and everything. I didn't know about it and I can *guarantee* you it was a murder. There was *no way* that guy woulda committed suicide, he had too much going for him. He *did not* wanna die. They said he died accidentally of asphyxiation with gasoline all inside the car, and he was dead when the car wasn't there? And Mrs. Fuller just checked half an hour before and there was no car there? And half an hour later after she checks it, she find her son in the car? Yeah, right."

"You know, my mother would not have missed the car being there. Not after Jack," says Randy, referring to the murder of their older brother. "She was worried about us all the time. That's why she was there with us. If something happened to Bobby somewhere else, which it did, and someone drove him back, which they did, they had to have known where we lived and where we parked the car. Mom didn't just look out the window, she went down there and walked the parking lot, several times that day. She had already become frantic about it. You know, it's just too much of a coincidence that this happened the night before we were gonna have the big break up meeting with Keene."

Twenty-two years after Bobby's death, a woman named Melody Dawson came forward to say she had spoken with him in the wee morning hours of July 18. Melody claimed that Loraine had called her about an hour before they found his body asking if Bobby had spent the night with her. She said that Bobby had received a phone call at 1 AM from a woman and that he had met some strange people from New York. She wanted to talk to Bobby about not breaking his contract. Larry Nunes had told her that the body had been placed in the car. What Melody said half matches Rick's recollection. Yes, he went to meet with a woman at 1 AM, and that woman was Melody herself, according to Rick.

Randy's wife Dale remembers Melody, "She was thirty-three years old at the time that she was part of the PJ's scene. She was from Chicago, like Paul Raffles and the others. She was supposed to kind of keep an eye on Bobby. I think she was supposed to have been good friends with Larry Nunes' wife. Randy said they always used to come into PJ's together, the three of them. And I think she was a call girl. Somebody out there knows something. Mrs. Fuller told me that she had a bad feeling about when Bobby left that night. She's the kind of person who's up all night long. So she said she kept going downstair, looking for the car and it wasn't there, and she'd go back up and she'd go back down and she'd pace. And then, from what I understand, when they saw the time of death—now I might not be right about this, but he couldn't have possibly driven himself back dead. Okay, so somebody had to have driven him back there. 'Cause according to what she said, the car wasn't there just five minutes before. And don't you think it's strange—okay, they're having this meeting, 'cause the band's gonna break up, you know, all this stuff's going on."

"They roughed Bobby up *bad*, and then he got in the car," Randy theorizes. "They went back in the house and when they next went out the door, Bobby was still parked in their driveway. They go to look, and he's dead. They get in the car and drive him back to Sycamore, watch from the side street to be sure no one sees them, then they pull in, park, and leave. Simple as that. You could easily take the side streets from Mulholland Drive down to Sycamore, it's all quiet streets. I've done it myself in mid afternoon, like even now you can do it, and unless a camera is on you, no one would know. Nobody wanted Bobby dead, but if a person twice his size was working him over, it's not that hard to understand that things could have gone too far. Bobby had drank a few beers with Lloyd that night, before he got the call and left. Well I don't know who it was, but I just don't think that Bobby would've, in his right mind, killed himself like that, you know, in that manner for my mother's sake. Would've done it a different way. And he would've left a note, to her, if nothing else. He was set up when he got that phone call, and whoever did it had it mind to kill him, or hurt him real bad. The call was probably about what was going to happen at Monday's meeting. That said, Bobby had the opportunity to say what was on his mind to whoever he was meeting with. Mustang was a one trick pony, and Bobby was the pony who was kicking up sand, ready to bolt from the stable. That's why I believe a detective was hired to prove that it was something more than suicide, possibly believing that accidental death would pay off as double indemnity. The meeting was the next day and he was called the night before. The gas thing had to have happened somewhere else, because his body had absorbed so much gasoline by that time."

"I drove my Corvette to Sycamore, came down Franklin, turned left, and then pulled into the parking lot," says Randy. "It was dirt, just a vacant lot. Somebody must have driven in there and left the car. Nobody saw anything. If *he* had driven it there, it would've had to have been a long time before rigor mortis set in. But rigor mortis had already set in when they found him, so somebody would have had to not see that car all day long to get rigor mortis *there*. But see, the thing is, she went out so many times to go look, that he couldn't possibly have been in full rigor mortis when she found him. Because the car wasn't there all that time. It just doesn't make any sense, her looking for it, completely worried after what had happened to Jack. She was *frantic* to find him, because he wasn't there. She had already been through it, twice, really. And twice she had had that premonition, so she was looking, I don't want to say it, but she was frantic. Bobby knew all about gasoline, that the lead would kill you. He knew all about gas. But then if you sat there and sniffed gasoline, it will make you *sick* before it kills you, knock you out. But see, that's what they say, maybe he was sniffing gas, backed out and just knocked the can over and suffocated. So that's where you get your accidental death. You can sniff it through a tube. I did one time and he told me that was bad for me, 'cause it's got lead in it. So I didn't do it anymore. I believe he either went to get gas *for* somebody who was *outta* gas, or *claimed* to be, and that coulda been up there on Mulholland. But I think that's where the gas comes in. It was there as a set-up to get him there. 'I'm outta gas, come and bring a gas can.' Well, I was in shock driving that car home. You know, just staring ahead. We couldn't talk, all of us were sitting there, and the smell, it was just incredible. We were just *numb*. They tried to clean out that smell, you know, leave the windows down when we were driving. Every time I smell gas, I think of that. Yeah, when we were kids, we were just doing it for experimenting, breathing from the gas can. Kids do things like that. We were only eight or nine years old. Bobby was smart enough to know, 'Hey, there's lead in that, don't do that,' so we didn't do it. Not to say that if he knew that, he couldn't have used it to kill himself. But bad things were happening, quitting the

job in Frisco. On the airplane, I thought this flying saucer had landed. God's throne, you know Ezekiel, God's throne was the highly polished prize. Ezekiel saw the wheel. That *was* a spaceship. Somebody was trying to build their way to salvation, and they said, 'God won't like that, and he'll destroy anybody trying to climb to heaven or fly to heaven to get away from what we're put here for, to overcome... Satan.' Man, I don't know. We've been through all of this so many times. And you know, if somebody called him and said they were out of gas, he had his slippers on and hurried and got out of there. That phone call had to be for gas. What else would the gas can be for? It's what I've been saying all along. How else are you gonna set him up? 'Come up here, we wanna talk to you and kick your ass?' I think somebody called and said, 'I'm out of gas, can you bring a can of gas?' Set him up, got him up there and beat the hell out of him and knocked him down that hill. Bobby would not reveal a lot of things. One time somebody asked me, 'Why is Bobby so optimistic about everything? Everything's gonna work out all the time? You're gonna get yourself in some trouble pullin' this shit.' And we're not dealing with people from El Paso. We're dealing with Mafia, we're dealing with big guys here. Everybody who owns a radio station is run by the mob. And recording industries, all of those were run by big people who were in the mafia, or in a mob of some kind, and money was the root of it all. Bobby could've been scared to death but wouldn't have talked to any of us about what was coming down. He could've been scared to tell my mother, to hurt her, scare her. But the gas can is the key to the answer of this. And why did he have a gas can? Did he pick it up because of the phone call? I think somebody had called him and said they were out of gas. And that could've been, 'I'll be right back, pick up a can of gas, give it to the guy. I'll be right back.' He came back dead with a can of gas."

I FOUGHT THE LAW

Lloyd Esinger, the building superintendant, was the last person to have professed to have seen Bobby alive. Says Randy, "The only thing I ever knew about Lloyd was that he liked to party. LSD, for sure, and pot. I didn't want to get busted so I didn't hang around him much, you know, from my experience from getting busted at the Zaragosa/El Paso border. He was in his late twenties, early thirties, light hair. Dewayne and I were laying around the pool one Saturday night at the apartment, getting ready for a gig at PJ's that night. We hear *Psst! Psst!* We looked up and this Lloyd guy is waving at us from his third floor apartment window for us to come up to have a beer. So there was a lot of people up there and some how I ended up in the bedroom of this Lloyd guy's place, rolling joints. I sent a girl out to get Dewayne to get him high. He had tried pot once before but didn't get high—he probably didn't inhale, like some people we know—so I said take a hit off this shit and tell me that! We left laughing our asses off! Lloyd opened the door when we were walking down the hall and he said, 'See you boys later,' as he waved kind of girly-like and we laughed even harder. When we went to our apartment, Dewayne got paranoid because my mother kept looking directly into his eyes trying to see why he was acting strange. Of course it didn't help that I was behind my mother, running my head up and down the side of the door edge to look like I didn't have a body. That night at PJ's was a trip because good old Dewayne said his kick drum felt like it was in slow motion and Bobby freaked him out every time he asked him what was wrong. Back to Lloyd, he was questioned by the police but I don't think they found out anything more that that he was definitely gay!"

"Bob used to drive us crazy because he would never open up and tell you what was really going in his head," said Randy. "The meeting that morning was supposed to be about all of us being pissed off about playing shit gigs as if they were just using us to get their share of the dough! When we were on tour, Jim, Dalton and I would get together and constantly bitch about how everything was all about Bobby and how we were just sidemen. I tried to reason with my brother about this in New York and his comment was that when we got back to LA, he was going out on his own. He also said that if they didn't let him out of the contract he would just quit Del-Fi and go back and open another teen club in El Paso. The meeting was to get us all back together and find out if the BF4 was going to survive. Bobby talked to other producers, Ahmet Ertegun from Atlantic, Phil Spector, Norman Petty, and probably more but I don't recall what he said to them. Ahmet Ertegun had something to do with it. He came out to a show. I met him at that time in New York, we all met him, at Ondine. I didn't go anywhere with him. Bobby did. I know we met Tommy James. Business stuff that got done was done without the band. They took Bobby out to do a lot of things that the band didn't get invited to. In Hollywood, same thing. A lot of questions I can't even answer. I might not have even met Tommy James, except for Bobby. It was a quick, 'Hello, I'm Bobby Fuller and this is Tommy James,' and there I am standing in the background with Jim and Dalton. The Gorham was where we stayed because they wouldn't let us stay at the Plaza like Keene. We got off at the Plaza and unloaded all of our equipment, and they came out and told us we couldn't stay there because the Rolling Stones had fans that trashed the hotel, running up and down the halls and everything. They wouldn't let us stay there, no more bands. I didn't meet the Rolling Stones, but we saw them running down the halls and stuff. They passed us by. Bobby was meeting with people we knew nothing about. There are lots of times when things are on the fire and it looks like stuff is gonna happen and for one reason or another, it doesn't. That apparently was—I don't remember the exact details, but you have to deal through agencies on those tours. The agencies, a lot of it depends on who they're going to open for, they would be going as the second act. There would have to be a headliner 'cause they weren't big enough for a headliner. Sometimes the major act will say, 'No, I don't want these guys as my second,' because maybe they're too strong. Know what I'm saying? And they'd make the lead act look bad. Sometimes that happens. You know, there's a lot of reasons why things get cancelled, but I never remembered it being a real definite thing, getting them going over to Europe. I don't remember it being a real deal breaker, catastrophic situation. Bobby was tough to work for. I mean, he was kind of a perfectionist, and he was also a loner, he wasn't a very outgoing guy. So apparently the guys felt that he wasn't really on their side. As a matter of fact, there were other things that came to my attention, where he was planning to go out as a single. And he was going to can the band and go as a single and had been negotiating with some other people which I didn't know anything about. There was no chance at that meeting that everything was gonna be okay. We weren't going to take any more gigs. Bobby was sick of all of it. We were gonna break up. Bobby was gonna go on his own because he wanted to play shows and things for the young and do the things we used to do, and not end up a club band, and that happens, as good as a band can be, they turn into a club band. Because they can't do nothing original, or aren't *allowed* to, and that's what they tried to make us, just that sterile type of thing, where we play the same thing over and over and over. We didn't really think it would end, you know? We were in a dream world, not facing reality. But Bobby knew we had to, and he had made his mind up that he was going to

I FOUGHT THE LAW

LEFT: *Bashin' back in El Paso;*
RIGHT: *Randy looking sharp*

end it. Because it was just too much *pressure* that I caused him, and that we all caused with the constant battle of 'we all want to be recognized as much as you.' And I think that it really hurt Bobby tremendously. After a while, he probably couldn't stand it. You know, my attitude, my anger about it and throwing a fit every time we played a show 'cause I didn't like the clothes we were wearing and whatever, and I think that really hurt—but in turn, I felt that I had reason to do that, I really did. Because it was just awful, actually. It was like being in hell, playing and thinking you're doing something , and all of the sudden it's given to one man and the rest of them are just side men. And here you had this feeling like the Beatles. We're all gonna be like this. A band. And they just tore that right out of the whole picture, you know? Just took it all from you. I'm not one who can be in the same band all my life. You know, I gotta make changes or just do my own thing because I don't want that myself, and I know Bobby didn't want it. It's always an ego trip. It's always somebody wanting to get on top of you. It's always—you know, if you're the main attraction of the band, then everyone is jealous. It happens every time. It's not only musicians, it's everybody. And when they get a little taste—and they don't get enough attention, they crave attention And then you've got a real problem. You've got a problem with this guy who's a fanatic about getting attention, like me, because I never got any. Bobby got it all! It was destroying me just like it was destroying him. With my anger and, 'You're gettin' all', and throwing records at Bob Keene and having a fit about everything. I was pissed off at Keene, because the main thing we had told him was that we were a *group*, all together. We were then. Not 'Bobby Fuller and group,' or 'Bobby Fuller and side men,' or nothin' else. And then I'd say, 'Well when are we gonna be recognized? The rest of us?' And you know, I'm fighting this battle with my own brother. And it shouldn't have been like that. They made it that way, and believe it or not, all the people who knew Bobby made it that way with me. Not just Bob Keene, not just Jim Reese, it was everybody from El Paso, because everything I ever heard was, 'Oh, you're Bobby's brother.' Well, you know, that's all I ever heard. And it didn't matter what I did, it was never good enough. I couldn't never figure myself out. After Bobby died I couldn't do anything for myself. Bobby was the one who always talked to Keene, to Nunes. I was the one getting in trouble. All the girls loved him. My self esteem was so low, with my family in El Paso, I could never do anything right. 'Your brother was so great,' people would say. When I turned twenty-eight years old, I had a breakdown and went to a therapist. I had no where to go. I started running down the street. They'd say, 'What's wrong with Randy?' I told my good friend Andy that I was gonna go kill myself. Nobody can help me. So I went for help and the first day they told me, 'You are not going off the deep end. You have a lot of anger. Get a punching bag and pound on it the best you can.' I did that for about ten years. Sometimes I still need it."

"My dad was always reading the Bible," continues Randy. "We would go to church on Easter Sunday, but I think my mother kinda lost faith in God after everything started happening. My dad was a Methodist. He would sit in a chair for hours and read the Bible, at least twice a week, maybe more. And I think he had faith, but he was a sinner like us all. But he still believed. I think Bobby was losing his faith, I think he was becoming Atheist. When we're young, we think there's something more out there for us. California has always been the dream of anybody in the Midwest or from a one-horse town like El Paso, where you don't have nothing to do, the sand's blowing and it's lonely. You go out in the desert, just sand blowin' across the highway. It's a lonely feeling. You know, maybe a coyote will just hobble across the freeway, and man, you can just feel the knives, and you just wanna freak out, you're so lonely. And I'd drive somewhere, anywhere, just for something to do. Something. Anything."

"Bobby didn't like me smokin' pot. Back then you'd take a diet pill the doctor gave you, there were no med tabs or all this. You didn't have that kind of stuff then. Bobby took pills the doctor gave him, and this girl Amber started him on it. Back then, it was a diet pill. Like Dexamil spansules, Christmas trees. He didn't need to alter his consciousness. It was already altered. He told me he had already taken LSD, and it didn't do anything for him. I said, 'Well you must have got some of that sugar cube shit.' Now and then, you would get some with a real mild dose of it. I said, 'If you take some of the stuff I took, you'll be lucky if they can scrape your brain up off the sidewalk with a scalpel.' He said, I'm gonna take it again, we're gonna go to the beach, and there's gonna be a psychologist there to keep everybody in control. I said, 'Well, that's good. But that stuff does not work for everybody, even with a psychologist there. It can put you in a place that you don't wanna be, and you can't get out of it for ten years or more, without help.' And I said, 'just let me be with you, or let me go if your going to do it so I can look after you.' He says, 'Okay.' And that's how that got started, 'cause that's what I told everybody, that he was gonna. And he said he was never gonna take it that night or the next night, I wasn't sure. But that was only a day or two before his death. Bobby would not have asked me to go along with him, with Melody or whoever went, to any LSD party. 'Cause he didn't realize what he was gonna get into, number one, and he didn't want me around, number two. He had his own thing going. I'm not sure about the LSD thing, but if he did take it, he could have fallen and gotten knocked out, got put in the car and driven home because they don't wanna get busted. That's what the whole thing has been all this time. That's what everybody thought including myself. I believe that when they called, because of the gas can, somebody called and said, 'I'm outta gas. You got a gas can?' Why else would you have a gas can in the car? Unless they're gonna burn the body, but then why drive him back to burn the body? If they were a little more professional, they wouldn't be stumbling around with a gas can. He was still alive when that gas can got into the car. They would have messed him up. He had full rigor mortis and that thing had been there all day. It was there from the word go. The biggest mystery is bringing the car back and parking it there. To this day, it could have just been an accident. Somebody got mad, they fought and they were so scared out of their wits – for what I'd do to them for one thing – and took the car there. Bobby was good to a lot of women. Made 'em think they were somebody. He was good at that. And he didn't do it for any predatory type of a thing, you know, to get women, 'cause I saw him around a lot of girls that he never put a make on, he just made 'em feel good. Well, that night, after he died, I had this vision that he died from a fall. Hurt or something, some kind of fall, knocked down, knocked over a balcony, knocked down somewhere. And put back in the car down there. Maybe it was an accident! I saw them bring Bobby's body out of the car. I saw him layin' in the seat. When I got there, I saw all these people out there—cops, ambulance, everything. I got there really quick, my mother called and said, 'Bobby's dead.' I was on Sunset Blvd. on the East Side, but I was there fast. I can't imagine he was on LSD that night. I don't think anybody could imagine on LSD that gas is some neat thing. I don't know, maybe they could. Maybe he was on LSD and thought that was some *nice smellin' good drinkin' stuff*. I've heard a lot of weird shit and I've done a lot of weird shit, but I woulda *never* drank gasoline, or I woulda never taken it again. They think he smothered to death from the fumes, sniffing it with a hose. I never heard anything about how they found gas in his blood or anything, or in his stomach. They didn't test for LSD. But they sure didn't spend much time on the car. I took the car back in a few days, and if it were homicide, they woulda kept the car. Went through it with a fine-toothed comb. But they decided it was a suicide. And then my dad went to pick up my uncle Charles at the airport. He had some knives on him that he made, had

some guns and things and they got pulled over coming back from the airport, found those knives and stuff in the trunk, I don't know why they got pulled over. I heard someone mouthed off, 'You dirty Texans, go back to Texas!' And my uncle Charles told one of them, 'I'll cut your damn—off!' They pulled him over and handcuffed my dad and handcuffed him, and my dad had all this stress and was handcuffed. Uncle Charles made all that stuff because he was kind of nutty, but he would never kill nobody. But they went to the police department, my dad and uncle Charles, to talk to the chief of police. And he kept telling him that this was a murder and you need to do something about it and the chief of police told him, 'If you know what's good for you, you'll keep your mouth shut.' That was the last of that. And he kept saying, 'There's something the matter, this was murder. This was murder. He didn't commit suicide.' He kept goin' on and on until that cop told him to shut up. They hired a private detective. He said that he'd run across some people that told him, 'You'd better watch it or you'll get yourself in *a lot* of trouble.' He'd probably been going around talking to the mob and stuff, different people. And then there's the speculation that Charlie Manson did it. Jim's wife Beth Reese said that Manson had come into PJ's and had asked for Bobby. He supposedly was asking Bobby for guitar lessons and stuff. I just can't imagine anyone drinking gas or smelling it and sitting in a hot car all day to kill himself. I drove the car back and I think the keys were either on the floorboard or the ignition. I had a really strong premonition back then in those days that it happened on Mulholland Drive, up at the top there. It was kind of wild there. At that time, you could get right up there into the sticks. And I had a feeling that he had been kinda knocked down a hill, like thrown down of something, or fell down it, even fell down it on acid or something. You can definitely hurt yourself real bad. And that's how he got the this and that and bein' wild and everybody all hopped up, 'We gotta get him home. He's out cold, we don't want anybody to know we're up here doin' this. Take him home, leave him in that car. The gas was in there, maybe they didn't even know or realize. Because *I think* that the phone call he got was somebody was outta gas, to bring the gas. Either *he* was outta gas, went to get the can at the gas station, walked to get it, something. There was a dentist was up there on Mulholland Drive, and that dentist was friends with Bob Keene. And I'm not so sure that Bobby didn't hang around that dentist with Melody and stuff in that area. We went to his house to watch the Beatles at the Hollywood Bowl, 'cause it overlooked the Hollywood Bowl. We could see, from his backyard—you couldn't really see 'em that well, 'cause it's quite a ways, but you could see the crowd and you could see them, but you could hear 'em real good 'cause the crowd was yellin' the other way. Bobby could've either gone to an acid party up there on Mulholland, or he went up there where Bob Keene was or something, 'cause they called him to come up there for a minute, and something happened, right there. And that's why it was so close to home, you know, he coulda been easily brought back. Because he fell down that thing, they were doin' acid, they had drugs, they didn't want anybody to know that they were the cause for him to fall down there and be hurt. But he wasn't dead, they put him in a car, drove him home and left. That's what my premonition was all those years. And I drove up there to the end of Mulholland Drive so many times that it'd make your head spin, lookin', trying to find a sign, but I never did. But I did find the place where I thought he fell down that I thought was it in my psychic visions.

   Right after Bobby died, I was at my friend Andy's house and we dropped some acid. We were looking into each other's

I FOUGHT THE LAW

eyes just as deep as we could. We said, 'Let's look as far as we could into each other's eyes and see what we can see.' And all of a sudden he turned into Bobby, cell to cell with an aura around him and he was trying to talk to me. Andy fell to the floor. It did something to him. To this day, I don't know if we were hallucinating or if it really happened. It was so strong. I was into the first acid trips around there and I was one of the pioneers of that. Well, you know the Byrds kind of started that, the acid thing.

As far as the music business goes, I think Bobby had his mind made up that he was getting out of this thing with Keene. If he was gonna step back and quit for awhile, he was gonna do that. I don't think he wanted to. Even if he wasn't gonna play, what's Bob Keene gonna do, sue him? What's he gonna get? What I knew about Bob Keene, if you didn't have any money, he didn't sue you. He could have stopped Bobby from making more records, but he couldn't stop him from going back to El Paso and opening another teen club and that's what Bobby would have done.

All we knew is we signed a contract as a group. It was different than Bobby's contract. There was a $100,000 insurance policy on the group and an $800,000 policy on Bobby. That just shows you what they think of the band and that's the big problem. It was all a lot of stress and 'are we gonna amount to anything?' It's all about you. It still is. This has been the main thing all along. It's awful weird about the timing of all this – the LSD days, the mob days, the corrupt police department. You can't get a definite yes or no about any of it and the police department doesn't have the records anymore. What the hell did we know back then to ask? If it was now, we'd be there. We'd know."

"Jim Reese hated Bobby," says Randy, "Bob Keene had a Jaguar XKE and he sold it to Jim and Jim was making payments and once all this came to an end, he couldn't make the payments. And so Bobby sold his blue Corvette and took over the payments on Jim's car. I started to get distant from Bobby around that time. He was down in the crack of the seat and there was blood. When they pulled his body out, he came out head first from the driver's side. The girls or Ricky made the call to the police and my mother called me. She was not in her right mind. We were all despondent. We were boys crying in our beer 'What are we gonna do?' Jim was all messed up because he was maybe going into the service but he got outta that. Myself, I think Bobby was hurt. There were skin slips. See, Bobby wasn't street smart. When I walk into a club and see a bad ass, I know he's a bad ass and want nothing to do with him. I have a sixth sense about that. Bobby didn't. We pulled out of that job in San Francisco. We were a teenybopper band. We had enough of those guys. Larry Nunes and Martin Goodman put up a lot of money and they lost a bunch. Bob Keene wasn't happy. Maybe some Manson guys were after Reese. He wouldn't give them guitar lessons and neither would Bobby."

Bobby Fuller was laid to rest four days after his death. A funeral service was held at 11 AM on Friday, July 22 at Church of the Hills Methodist Church in Hollywood and burial was at Forest Lawn Cemetary. Phil Spector was the first of the bereaved to approach the casket. He had also been the first to send Bobby a congratulatory opening night telegram at PJ's, right before Ahmet Ertegun's message came in via Western Union. Phil told this writer that Bobby was "a real talent" and "a great guy". "I miss him," he had added, looking meditatively into the distance. Keene had told Bobby to avoid Spector at all costs, calling him "a freak" and a man with "dubious business practices." Bob Keene and Larry Nunes, who served as pallbearers with Jim, Dalton, Paul Politi and Rick Stone, sent flowers signed "Bob and Larry, Stars Of Tomorrow." Pamela was there. Barry White. Friends from El Paso. Hollow-eyed fan clubbers. Paul Raffles and the PJ's crew. The casket was lowered into the earth at Forest Lawn Cemetary at Hollywood Hills, where Bobby now keeps company with slumbering neighbors ranging from Liberace to Ozzie, Harriett, and Ricky Nelson.

"Mother was a vegetable after that, " says Randy. "We took her to the cemetery one last time the next day. She fell on the grave and you just couldn't get her off. We had to drag her to the car. We had to get out of there."

Hours after the funeral, Bob Keene called Lawson Fuller, asking him to come by the office. There were debts that he claimed that we owed him. Bobby had something like $16,000 in an account and they wanted that money, and they paid the funeral and everything out of it, out of Bobby's own money. All of the equipment, amps, guitars, the microphones and the stands, and everything else, he claimed were his. I called him up and told him that I wanted to get my brother's stuff out of there, and he said, 'Well Bobby owed me money and that's staying here,' and then he wouldn't answer the phone after that. So I called up his wife Elsa and told her if he wasn't downstairs in ten minutes, I was gonna shoot. I told her I had my scope, my deck, and my gun, which I did. He was down there in ten minutes, just like that. I got Bobby's stuff and got the hell out of there."

An autopsy had been conducted by twenty-four year old Loma Linda Medical School graduate Jerry W. Nelson, MD, a Los Angeles County Deputy Medical Examiner. Chief Medical Examiner-Coroner Theodore Curphey, and his immediate underling Thomas Noguchi (who would inherit the position fifteen months later) were more than likely involved with similar detailing on Chief Parker, whose celebrity death and funeral preceded Bobby's by two days, respectively. Nelson's final verdict, three months after the fact, was "Asphyxia due to inhalation of gasoline. Final 10-17-66, released 10-18-66." That said, the real question was, when did he die, and where. Rigor mortis begins three to four hours after death, with the body stiffening over a period of twelve to eighteen hours, when maximum stiffness can be observed. Hot temperatures speed up the average time frame.

Thermometers in Los Angeles on Monday, July 18 peaked at noon at 75.9 degrees Fahrenheit, with nine hours of the day registering over 70 degrees. In a closed automobile, temperatures rise up to twenty degrees higher than that outside of the vehicle. That said, should rigor been accelerated (or not), they would not have been able to pull his body out of the car feet first. It would have been inflexible, "stiff" as the slang expression for rigor dictates. Had he died seated in the car in the late night or early morning hours, removing him from the vehicle would have been a challenge. He could not have been extracted, "slid out head first," as recalled by eyewitnesses. Extensive blistering and peeling of skin were observed on the skin of the face, neck, anterior chest, upper and lower extremities, and back. Head Toxicologist Edward R. Thompson submitted a Report of Chemical Analysis for the Los Angeles County Medical Examiner-Coroner's office at the Hall of Justice on July 25, 1966—blood was absent of Barbiturates, Ethanol (alcohol), carbon monoxide, Doriden, Meprobamate, Phenacetin, Valium, Librium, Cyanide, Chlorinated hydrocarbons, and strychnine, all absent.

The death remained uninvestigated by the LAPD. As no foul play was noted in the police report, the car was not impounded, and no criminal investigation was undertaken. Bobby's death occurred at a bad time, as though any other time

I FOUGHT THE LAW

would have been better. The head of the LAPD, Police Chief William H. Parker had died unexpectedly of a heart attack while giving a speech on Saturday night, July 16. On Monday July 18, the day that Bobby's body was discovered, Chief of Detectives, Thad Brown—who had headed the LA detective bureau since 1949—was sworn in as acting police chief to replace Parker. Chief Parker's body lay in state that day from 2-4 PM in the City Hall rotunda, with a full military funeral scheduled for Wednesday, July 20 at St Vibiana's Cathedral. Every officer of any sort of rank was present at the memorial and funeral—the city government was in a state of shock. Parker was the longest serving police chief and had been on the force thirty-nine years, and was Jack Webb's real life inspiration for *Dragnet*'s Sgt Friday. He was followed in Chiefdom by Thad Brown, who with Parker, was deeply involved in the non-solving of the Black Dahlia murder case. Strangely, during Parker's laying in state, Thad Brown personally selected rookie cop Officer Steve Hodel to pose for a photograph. The young officer was the son of Dr. George Hodel, associate of both Brown and Parker, who had been the prime suspect in the Black Dahlia murders, only to have remained uncharged. Steve Hodel was asked by this writer if he recalled that day with Thad Brown, or events in Los Angeles in the days immediately preceding Parker's passing. He agreed that it was hectic. A hundreds-strong, miles-long motorcade wound down the funeral route from downtown LA to the San Fernando cemetery where he was laid to rest. The Detective Bureau was in flux, having to replace Brown, as he moved up into place as the new Chief. And here we had Bobby Fuller, whose death and funeral followed Parker's by two respective days—the worst possible timing for a murder investigation.

Bob Keene claims that he hired private investigators to change the cause of death from "suicide" to "accidental." Presumably this was done to allow life insurance to pay off. But did it, and did it matter? California life insurance code specifically excludes "death by poison, gas, or fumes, unless they are the direct result of an occupational accident." One week after Bobby's death, Larry Nunes and Morris Levy announced their Roulette/ITCC pact in a full page *Billboard* ad. Eighteen months later, Privilege/Tip Top would be sold lock, stock and barrel to Transcontinental Investment Corporation/Transcontinental Music Corporation. Jim Reese remembered going by the Stereo Fi office and seeing a dumpster stacked and strewn with files and office furniture, stationery blowing into the street. It was an unceremonious end to a fast and furious run. Tip Top got the final box lots of Mustang returns, as they had from the start, buying them for three cents a record and selling them, royalty-free, for half a buck apiece on cut-out racks. Jim said the hallways at Stereo-Fi were lined with boxes of Bobby Fuller Four albums, ready for the cut-out racks at Montgomery Ward and other fine chains and record discounters. Bob Keene would go on to sell home security systems.

PJ's would never the same. Paul Raffles ended up in debt, a troubled man. Donalie Young recalled," I heard he blew his brains out. Poor Paul. He had probably been in bed too long with some of the guys from the Green Mile." The brain blowing occurred in 1973, the same year that Eddie Nash took on PJ's, beginning a new era for the venue, with a name change to the Starwood. Life went on in Hollywood, for some. Mia Farrow, who had danced at PJ's to the beat of the BF4, (and who had received her first drum lesson from Dewayne), married PJ's enthusiast Frank Sinatra the day after Bobby's death. Future Manson acolyte Bobby Beausoleil and his band the Outfit was making a racket at the Dragon A Go-Go on the heels of the BF4 blowing out of San Francisco in a contract-breaking huff.

The death of Bobby Fuller in July of 1966 marked the end of an era. At the age of twenty-three, the rock and roll career of the unbelievable, irresistible Bobby Fuller was over, and with it, the wide-eyed optimism that marked the West Texas sound of the "Rock and Roll King Of The Southwest," which rings as honest and true today as it did fifty years ago. It always will.

UNPUBLISHED INTERVIEW WITH BOBBY AND RANDY FULLER 1966

Don Paulsen, editor of Charlton Publications' *uber*-hip *Hit Parader* magazine, conducted a taped interview with Bobby and Randy Fuller at the *HP* offices at 529 Fifth Avenue in New York City in the Spring of 1966 when they were on their East Coast tour. By this time, Bobby is openly admitting his admiration for British groups, although standing by his Texas roots. This is the first publication of this interview. It begins with Don asking the brothers about the beginnings of the BF4.

BOBBY: We all played in separate groups around town and decided to get together. Most of the other members of those groups got jobs and things. Some guys stick with it. Some guys find out it's a lot harder to be a musician than people really think. People protest musicians but they just don't know better. We put out about ten records before we got one that did anything. We went to California from El Paso because we couldn't go any farther in El Paso. We met Bob Keene who I'd met three years before. He told me to go back and work and come back. I did. We had three records out on Mustang before *I Fought The Law*. Before that we had three or four on our labels, Eastwood and Exeter, our own record company.

Mustang built a studio for us where we could go in any

time we want to. I helped put things in there – an Ampex eight track recorder, equalizers, three echo chambers and an echo chamber I developed myself.

Our sound is West Texas rock and roll with our touch. It's a border sound. We take sounds from Mexico with maracas, one time we used a bottle. And little finger cymbals. We hear sounds live that aren't really there. We have to duplicate them in the studio because the microphones don't pick them up.

RANDY: When you have the interaction between the amps we use and the way we play our guitars, there's certain harmonics that we hear but the microphones don't pick them up, so we pick up bottles and stomp our feet.

I heard *I Fought The Law* on a Crickets album. About five years ago And we started playing it and released a version in El Paso. It went to Number Two on KELP. The only thing that beat it out was a song called *A Hard Day's Night*. So we waited and recut it and released it in Hollywood and it went to Number Nine in the nation.

BOBBY: I like the Beatles and the Animals. My favorite singer is John Lennon, and my favorite songwriters are Lennon/McCartney, Burt Bacharach, and Tony Hatch. For TV shows, I like *I Spy* and *Run For Your Life*. I like extremely feminine girls.

RANDY: I like steak and broads.

BOBBY: Who helped us the most? Bob Keene, our "big daddy" and Larry Nunes. I remember the first time we came to New York. I mean, I dig flying but he started talking about plane crashes and I got scared to death but I didn't tell anybody. He got me extremely scared.

I FOUGHT THE LAW

RANDY: It's a frightening experience for young little Texas boys to come to New York.

BOBBY: I'd like to sit in with the Beatles to see if they'd excite me like they do on records, maybe play some songs they haven't yet recorded and see what they sound like.

RANDY: What quality do you look for in a girl? Small feet. Where do I like to go on a date? A motel. DON'T PRINT THAT!

BOBBY: I've had things happen in the last six years that wouldn't happen to most people. I lost a brother who was killed, stupid things like that. It had a direct bearing on our music, like the blues in our music.

I'd like to go to Hawaii. I'd like to conduct a symphony just one time, like the *William Tell Overture*. I try in writing to incorporate classical bearing, jazz, rock and roll. I like Stravinsky. Maurice Ravel's *Daphnis et Chloe* and *Bolero*. When I hear that, I go in another room and try to add to it. One song I wrote, *Never To Be Forgotten* and also *Let Her Dance* remind me of *Bolero*. I wish that somebody would take some of the music we've done and put it to a symphony orchestra just to see what it would sound like. I use a lot of major chords. I wouldn't know how to arrange it. I haven't had much education in composition. I know it'd sound wild! They did it with the Beatles and it came out real groovy. Brian Wilson did it, too.

We play for ages between thirteen and thirty. They all react the same. In LA, they're getting more excited. *I'm* getting more excited.

RANDY: Most people want to know why we don't sound as good on record as we do live. But we get excited when we play in front of people and drive, drive, drive.

BOBBY: We have to mix our records down for a mono single, but there's still separation. I don't like to listen to our group in stereo. It ruins the effect of rock and roll. It spreads it out too much. For rock and roll it should all come from the same place. A lot of engineers cut stereo wrong. The singers should be in the middle not on one side. The bass and the bass drum and the snare should all be in the center.

RANDY: The Yardbirds do that. There's about twenty groups that are going all weird because of LSD and marijuana. It's just a way of life for them.

IMHOTEP
QUO
VADIS

BOBBY AND RANDY FULLER DISCOGRAPHY

BOBBY FULLER You're In Love/Guess We'll Fall In Love (Yucca 141) 11/61

BOBBY FULLER You're In Love/Guess We'll Fall In Love (Yucca 141) 2/62

BOBBY FULLER Gently My love/My Heart Jumped (Yucca 144) 5/62

BOBBY FULLER Nervous Breakdown/Not Fade Away (Eastwood no #) 7/62

BOBBY FULLER Saturday Night/Stringer (Todd 1090) 10/63

BOBBY FULLER Wine, Wine, Wine/King Of The Beach (Exeter 122) 1/64

BOBBY FULLER She's My Girl/I Fought The Law (Exeter 124) 2/64

BOBBY FULLER AND THE FANATICS Fool Of Love/Shakedown (Exeter 126) 8/64

BOBBY FULLER AND THE FANATICS Those Memories Of You/Our Favorite Martian (Donna 1403) 12/64

SHINDIGS Wolfman/Thunder Reef (Mustang 3003) 12/64

BOBBY FULLER FOUR Take My Word/She's My Girl (Mustang 3004) 2/65

BOBBY FULLER FOUR Let Her Dance/Another Sad And Lonely Night (Mustang 3006) 5/65

BOBBY FULLER FOUR Let Her Dance/Another Sad And Lonely Night (Liberty 55812) 7/65

BOBBY FULLER FOUR Never To Be Forgotten/You Kiss Me (Mustang 3011) 9/65

BOBBY FULLER FOUR Let Her Dance/Another Sad And Lonely Night (Mustang 3012) 9/65

BOBBY FULLER FOUR Let Her Dance/Another Sad And Lonely Night (Roulette 4655) 1965 unreleased

BOBBY FULLER FOUR I Fought The Law/Little Annie Lou (Mustang 3014) 10/65

BOBBY FULLER FOUR Love's Made A Fool Of You/Don't Ever Let Me Know (Mustang 3016) 3/66

BOBBY FULLER FOUR The Magic Touch/My True Love (Roulette 4685) 1966 unreleased

BOBBY FULLER FOUR The Magic Touch/My True Love (Mustang 3018) 6/66

BOBBY FULLER FOUR It's Love, Come What May/It's Love, Come What May (Mustang 3020) 1966 unreleased

RANDY FULLER It's Love, Come What May/Wolfman (Mustang 3020) 8/66

KRLA KING OF THE WHEELS Never To Be Forgotten/Another Sad And Lonely Night/She's My Girl/Take My Word/Fool Of Love/Let Her Dance/King Of The Wheels/The Phantom Dragster/Saturday Night/KRLA Top Eliminator (Mustang 900) 10/65

I FOUGHT THE LAW Let Her Dance/Julie/A New Shade Of Blue/Only When I Dream/You Kiss Me/Little Annie Lou/I Fought The Law/Another Sad And Lonely Night/Saturday Night/Take My Word/Fool Of Love/Never To Be Forgotten (Mustang 901) 2/66

I FOUGHT THE LAW

RELATED

BOB TAYLOR AND THE COUNTS Taylor's Rock/Thunder (Yucca 102) 10/58

BOB TAYLOR AND THE COUNTS Child Of Fortune/Don't Be Unfair (Yucca 110) 4/59

JERRY BRIGHT AND THE EMBERS Almost Blue/Jim's Jive (Yucca 139) 10/61

JERRY BRIGHT AND THE EMBERS Be Mine/I'll Always Be (Yucca 143) 2/62

COUNTS Chug-A-Lug/Surfer's Paradise (Manco 1060) 7/63

CHANCELLORS Judy/I Can No Longer Pretend (Eastwood 120) 11/63

BILL TAYLOR AND THE SHERWOODS Just As I Love Her/You Hold My Letters (Not Me) (Eastwood 121) 11/63

SHERWOODS Tickler/Black Out (Exeter 123) 1/64

JERRY BRIGHT Indian River/Rosie (Bright no #) 4/64

PAWNS The Pawn/South Bay (Exeter 125) 8/64

THE PAWNS Lonely/ **DAVID HAYES** Meet Me Here (In New Orleans) (Exeter 127) 9/64

JOHNNY CRAWFORD Am I Too Young/Janie Please Believe Me (Del-Fi 4305) 8/65

JAY HORTON I Trip On You/I Wanna Dance (Mustang 3010) 8/65

POST 1966 DEL-FI/MUSTANG RANDY FULLER RELATED SINGLES

RANDY FULLER Revelation/It's Love Come What May (Show Town 366) 1968

I FOUGHT THE LAW

RANDY FULLER 1,000 Miles Into Space /1,000 Miles Into Space (Show Town 482) 1969

POTTERY OUTFIT Captain Zig-Zag/no flip (Edsel 777) 1969

LOS PAISANOS La Bamba/La Malaguena//Lil Maggie/Roddy McCorley/Los Mirlos/Bowling Green/Blowing In The Wind/500 Miles/Vaca Colorada/Cu Cu Ra/Yellow Bird/Torito (Exeter 101) 1964

BE SURE TO PICK UP ALL OF NORTON'S EL PASO ROCK ALBUMS...

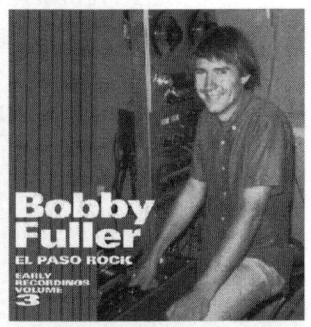

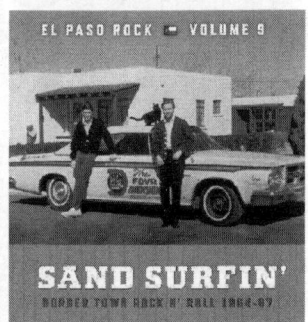

BOBBY FULLER
ON NORTON RECORDS!

IN PERSON
The One and Only
BOBBY FULLER
EL PASO'S OWN RECORDING STAR

Will make a Special Appearence
Friday, Sept. 28th, 1962
Dance from 8:00 p. m. to 12:00

Continental Ballroom

5 miles East Border Town Drive
Inn on the Carlsbad Highway.

★ U - ALL COME ★

In Memory of

ROBERT G. FULLER
1942 - 1966

Funeral Services

Friday   11:00 AM
July 22, 1966
in the
"CHURCH OF THE HILLS"
and interment
in
Forest Lawn Memorial Park
Hollywood Hills

Callanan Mortuary Directors

I FOUGHT THE LAW
(Sonny Curtis)

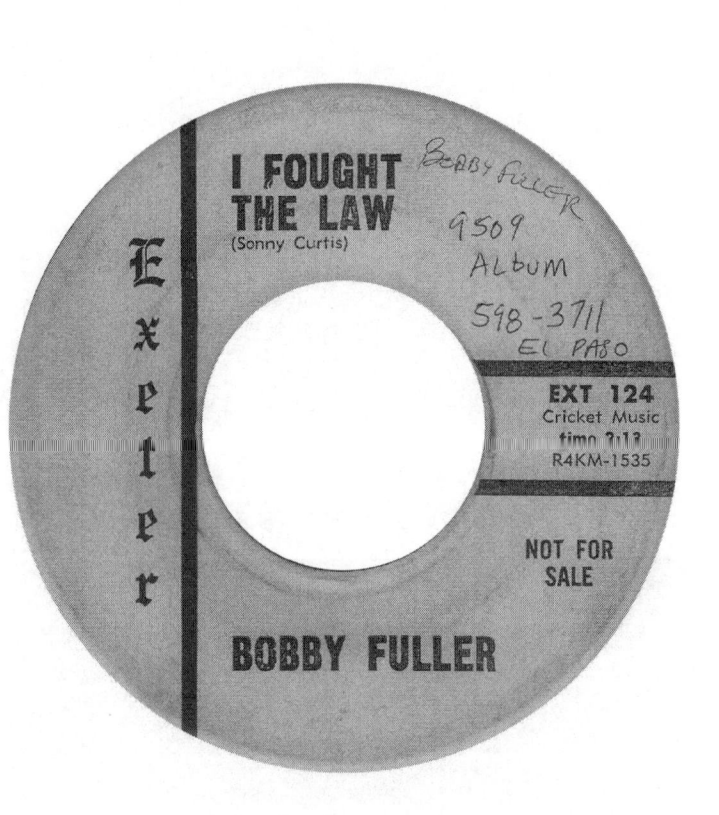

Exeter

BOBBY FULLER

EXT 124
Cricket Music
time 2:13
R4KM-1535

NOT FOR SALE

Handwritten: BOBBY FULLER 9509 ALBUM 598-3711 EL PASO